Kevin K. Kumashiro, PhD
Editor

Restoried Selves
Autobiographies of Queer Asian/ Pacific American Activists

Pre-publication
REVIEWS,
COMMENTARIES,
EVALUATIONS . . .

"The personal histories in this collection convincingly illustrate the delusive line between being and action. In most conventional coming-out narratives, queers often have to come to terms with their sexuality alone before they can act on any political implications of their orientation. The stories of these young women and men turn this narrative on its head. As people of color, oppression is a daily fact of life, and they cannot afford the luxury of this delay between identity and activism. Although their paths to activism varied in lengths and curves, it is in the very act of social justice that these brave souls discovered who they are. They were able to come out racially, sexually, and politically, only by placing themselves in the context of a community, even when relations in that community were, at times, uneasy. Just as important, young queers of color can learn from these stories that identity is not an end in itself, but an anchor for a broader power analysis that must drive any political struggle. By sharing their stores, the activists in this collection show the incredible role queer Asian/Pacific Americans have in linking struggles and building coalitions across communities."

Eric C. Wat
Author, *The Making of a Gay Asian Community: An Oral History of Pre-AIDS Los Angeles*

More pre-publication
REVIEWS, COMMENTARIES, EVALUATIONS . . .

"**R**estoried Selves is moving, spirited, and at times funny. Most important, the book is an important and timely political intervention. Asian/Pacific American activists narrate their lives not as tacit avowals of the LGBT identities but as a way to claim and locate their legitimate place in the public arena. 'Queerness' is given a specific set of voices and registers through these autobiographies. The twists and turns of each life story unravel the complexities of living on the margins of multiple communities and cultures complicated by immigration, homophobia, and racism. This book will be a source of inspiration and affirmation for other activists, scholars, and most of all, to young queer Asian/Pacific Americans who are searching for their own place in society."

Martin F. Manalansan IV, PhD
Assistant Professor,
Department of Anthropology,
University of Illinois,
Urbana–Champaign

"**R**estoried Selves: Autobiographies of Queer Asian/Pacific American Activists, edited by Kevin Kumashiro, is a collection of political-social-cultural-personal 'restories' (autobiographies) of queer APA activists from a wide range of activisms. Most are young activists, many were LGBT organizers in high school, college, or graduate school; several work today on the staff of various LGBT organiza-

tions. All tell a story from the trenches of LGBT activism as an organizer, writer, minister, psychologist, or teacher. All write tellingly from their multiple identities as a person who is queer, Asian/Pacific Islander or hapa, and immigrant or American-born/raised. Knowing some of the contributors and their long list of political accomplishments, I expected a retelling of activist struggles. Instead, I was pleasantly surprised to read an inside story of personal struggle that interlaced each political account. Through these stories I shared, if only for a short while, what it may be like to be a transgender or bisexual person of APA heritage. Especially poignant was Jeanette Mei Gim Lee's Good Friday queer commemoration to her congregation, which relates a touching story of her elderly Chinese grandmother. Loren Javier's reminiscences of a pained adolescence in the Midwest dealing with his intersexuality, homosexuality, and Asian American identity were gleefully dotted with references to familiar TV shows and movie stars. You will recognize many other authors such as Helen Zia, Al and Jane Nakatani, Wei Ming Dariotis, TC Duong, and Pauline Park; and those you don't know now you'll be pleased to meet in this wonderful new book."

Trinity A. Ordona, PhD
Associate Director,
Lesbian Health Research Center,
University of California, San Francisco

NOTES FOR PROFESSIONAL LIBRARIANS AND LIBRARY USERS

This is an original book title published by the Harrington Park Press®, an imprint of The Haworth Press, Inc. Unless otherwise noted in specific chapters with attribution, materials in this book have not been previously published elsewhere in any format or language.

CONSERVATION AND PRESERVATION NOTES

All books published by The Haworth Press, Inc. and its imprints are printed on certified pH neutral, acid free book grade paper. This paper meets the minimum requirements of American National Standard for Information Sciences-Permanence of Paper for Printed Material, ANSI Z39.48-1984.

Restoried Selves
Autobiographies of Queer Asian/ Pacific American Activists

HAWORTH Gay & Lesbian Studies
John P. De Cecco, PhD
Editor in Chief

Out of the Twilight: Fathers of Gay Men Speak by Andrew R. Gottlieb

The Mentor: A Memoir of Friendship and Gay Identity by Jay Quinn

Male to Male: Sexual Feeling Across the Boundaries of Identity by Edward J. Tejirian

Straight Talk About Gays in the Workplace, Second Edition by Liz Winfeld and Susan Spielman

The Bear Book II: Further Readings in the History and Evolution of a Gay Male Subculture edited by Les Wright

Gay Men at Midlife: Age Before Beauty by Alan L. Ellis

Being Gay and Lesbian in a Catholic High School: Beyond the Uniform by Michael Maher

Finding a Lover for Life: A Gay Man's Guide to Finding a Lasting Relationship by David Price

The Man Who Was a Woman and Other Queer Tales from Hindu Lore by Devdutt Pattanaik

How Homophobia Hurts Children: Nurturing Diversity at Home, at School, and in the Community by Jean M. Baker

The Harvey Milk Institute Guide to Lesbian, Gay, Bisexual, Transgender, and Queer Internet Research edited by Alan Ellis, Liz Highleyman, Kevin Schaub, and Melissa White

Stories of Gay and Lesbian Immigration: Together Forever? by John Hart

From Drags to Riches: The Untold Story of Charles Pierce by John Wallraff

Lyton Strachey and the Search for Modern Sexual Identity: The Last Eminent Victorian by Julie Anne Taddeo

Before Stonewall: Activists for Gay and Lesbian Rights in Historical Context edited by Vern L. Bullough

Sons Talk About Their Gay Fathers: Life Curves by Andrew R. Gottlieb

Restoried Selves: Autobiographies of Queer Asian/Pacific American Activists edited by Kevin K. Kumashiro

Queer Crips: Disabled Gay Men and Their Stories by Bob Guter and John R. Killacky

Dirty Young Me and Other Gay Stories by Joseph Itiel

Queering Creole Spiritual Traditions: Lesbian, Gay, Bisexual, and Transgender Participation in African-Inspired Traditions in the Americas by Randy P. Conner with David Hatfield Sparks

How It Feels to Have a Gay or Lesbian Parent: A Book by Kids for Kids of All Ages by Judith E. Snow

Restoried Selves
Autobiographies of Queer Asian/ Pacific American Activists

Kevin K. Kumashiro, PhD
Editor

HPP

Harrington Park Press®
An Imprint of The Haworth Press, Inc.
New York • London • Oxford

Published by

Harrington Park Press®, an imprint of The Haworth Press, Inc., 10 Alice Street, Binghamton, NY 13904-1580.

© 2004 by Kevin K. Kumashiro. All rights reserved. No part of this work may be reproduced or utilized in any form or by any means, electronic or mechanical, including photocopying, microfilm, and recording, or by any information storage and retrieval system, without permission in writing from the publisher. Printed in the United States of America.

Cover design by Lora Wiggins.

Cover illustrations:

Left: "homeland" (2001), graphite, color pencil, pens, markers. *Not being able to go home because of not knowing where home is.* Original artwork by Tokai Chigusa (Kobe).

Right: "rainy season" (2001), craypas, color pencil, graphite. *Change, coming like a rainstorm.* Original artwork by Tokai Chigusa (Kobe).

Library of Congress Cataloging-in-Publication Data

Restoried selves : autobiographies of queer Asian/Pacific American activists / Kevin Kumashiro, editor.
    p. cm.
Includes bibliographical references and index.
ISBN 1-56023-462-8 (alk. paper)—ISBN 1-56023-463-6 (softcover : alk. paper)
I. Kumashiro, Kevin K. 1970-

HQ75.7 R47 2003
305.895073—dc21

2002151325

To queer Asian/Pacific American youth

CONTENTS

ABOUT THE EDITOR

Kevin K. Kumashiro, PhD, is Director of the Center for Anti-Oppressive Education, where he produces resources for educators interested in creating and engaging in forms of education that challenge multiple oppressions. Dr. Kumashiro is editor of *Troubling Intersections of Race and Sexuality: Queer Students of Color and Anti-Oppressive Education,* and author of *Troubling Education: Queer Activism and Anti-Oppressive Pedagogy.*

Contributors

Pabitra Benjamin is an active young queer Nepali American woman who is constantly learning what "identities" mean in different societies and how to better diverse communities. A third-year undergraduate student in languages and cultures of Asia and sociology at the University of Wisconsin-Madison, Pabitra works with multiple student organizations to improve campus climate.

Tokai Chigusa (Kobe) is a twenty-one-year-old artist-activist and a senior majoring in visual arts with a concentration in Asian American studies at Oberlin College in Oberlin, Ohio. She identifies as a Japanese American boy-dyke; writes poetry and participates in poetry slamming; and enjoys short story writing, print making, photography, and graphic design. She is currently working on an Asian/Pacific American-dyke film, *Revolutionary Love*.

Nur-e-alam S. Chisty is currently a candidate for a bachelor's degree in psychology with a concentration in elementary education at Vassar College in Poughkeepsie, New York. After teaching elementary school for a few years, Nur-e-alam hopes to pursue graduate studies in antiracist and antihomophobic pedagogy in public schooling.

Lance Collins is twenty-one years old. Having received a bachelor's degree in political science at eighteen and a master's degree in indigenous politics at twenty from the University of Hawai'i at Manoa, Lance is currently studying at the University of Hawai'i William S. Richardson School of Law. He likes cuddling and sleeping.

Roland Sintos Coloma has worked as a university student affairs administrator, high school English teacher, and union and community organizer. A doctoral student at Ohio State University, Roland is researching nationalism and education within early twentieth-century U.S.-Philippines colonial relations. He runs, writes poetry, indulges in modern dance, and plays with his cat, Siopao.

Alain Anh-Tuan Dang received a Master of Arts degree from the Department of Urban Planning at UCLA, where he organized affirmative-action, domestic-partnership, and corporate-accountability campaigns. Currently living in Los Angeles, he enjoys running on the beach and karaoke.

Wei Ming Dariotis is Assistant Professor of Asian American studies at San Francisco State University, where she researches Asians of mixed heritage. Wei Ming advises the university's Hapa Club, facilitates the San Francisco Chapter of Hapa Issues Forum (www. hapaissuesforum.org), co-edited the Hapa issue of *Oriental Whatever* (#9), and is co-editing an anthology, *Bi Bi Grrrls: Bisexual/Biracial Women.*

TC Duong is the former East Coast Field Manager at PFLAG (Parents, Families, and Friends of Lesbians and Gays), where he worked to support PFLAG chapters on the East Coast as well as to support families of color across the country. TC lives with his partner, Jonathan Darr, in Washington, DC.

Loren R. Javier is the former Cultural Interest Media Manager at GLAAD (Gay & Lesbian Alliance Against Defamation). Loren has developed and presented a variety of media trainings and panels for and about lesbian, gay, bisexual, transgender, and questioning (LGBTQ) people of color, and in 1997, was named one of the "Best and Brightest Under 30" by *The Advocate.*

David C. Lee is a Chinese American living in Madison, Wisconsin. Having received a PhD in counseling psychology from the University of Wisconsin-Madison, David currently works in health care management. A former California lawyer, David is also a diversity facilitator and legal advisor. He misses good Chinese food.

Jeanette Mei Gim Lee is a Hapa Chinese American and white queer feminist. Currently in seminary at the Pacific School of Religion in Berkeley, California, Jeanette is a clergy candidate in the Universal Fellowship of Metropolitan Community Churches, a primarily GLBT Christian denomination.

Cristina M. Misa is a Chicana-Samoan lesbian activist and graduate student. She is pursuing a doctoral degree in the Department of Educational Policy Studies at the University of Illinois, Urbana-Champaign. Her research interests include the plight of queer students of color, specifically, Chicana/o and Pacific Islander students in public schooling.

Pauline Park is cofounder of Gay Asians and Pacific Islanders of Chicago, Iban/Queer Koreans of New York, Queens Pride House, the New York Association for Gender Rights Advocacy, the Out People of Color Political Action Club, and most recently, the Guillermo Vasquez Democratic Club of Queens. She has also served on the steering committee of Gay Asian & Pacific Islander Men of New York.

k. terumi shorb is a hapa Japanese/white composer, performer, writer, artist, and activist tranny-boy-fag-dyke born and raised in suburban Massachusetts, rural Niigata, Japan, and urban Tokyo. S/he writes music for social change mostly for people who are queer and/or of color. S/he believes that there is no such thing as art for art's sake.

Wendy M. Thompson is a young, bi-queer, Chinese/African-American poet and artist. Her written work has appeared in the anthologies, *Yell-Oh Girls* and *Running for their Lives,* and her video documentary, *stories from the blackasian planet,* was screened at Ladyfest Lansing and Mujerfest in 2002. Wendy resides in Riverside, California, where she is completing an undergraduate degree in Asian American studies.

"You Yun" was born and raised in China and came to the United States in the early 1990s. Her main training and work experiences are in mental health and education. She has been active in building the Chinese tongzhi communities both in China and the United States since 1995.

Helen Zia is author of the highly acclaimed book, *Asian American Dreams: The Emergence of an American People.* She is an award-winning journalist, a contributing editor to *Ms. Magazine,* a longtime activist for social justice issues, and the daughter of Chinese immigrants. Helen co-authored the story of Wen Ho Lee, who was falsely accused of being a spy for China, in *My Country Versus Me.*

Foreword

With this book, Kevin Kumashiro gives a group of gay, lesbian, bi-sexual, transgender, and self-identified "queer" Asian and Pacific Americans the opportunity to share not only their experiences grow-ing up, but also the ways those experiences have led them to become social activists. Their autobiographies do much to educate and in-spire readers to better understand and promote the acceptance and well-being of queer Asian and Pacific Americans. They also give us an opportunity to examine and reexamine each of our own percep-tions and feelings about queer Asian and Pacific Americans.

In a sense, their autobiographies are just another part of their ac-tivisms. By speaking out, they are defying and/or overcoming the familial and cultural constraints commonly placed on them to not "publicize" any aspect of their lives that can be a source of shame. After all, a code of silence often surrounds life experiences that may "implicate" their families, communities, and cultures with whatever may be construed as negative. These autobiographies raise ques-tions about the legitimacy of those familial and cultural expecta-tions and values that often force queer Asian and Pacific Americans to reinforce the code of silence and impose shame upon themselves because of the nature of their sexual orientation.

Asian and Pacific American families and cultures must do every-thing possible to understand, embrace, and include members of our families who are queer. Too many Asian and Pacific American chil-dren who are growing up queer do so without familial and cultural support. They often grow up fearful, confused, closeted, and alien-ated, and although they are dependent on their parents, siblings, and other family members for their well-being, they do not turn to them because they do not want to disappoint, shame, or dishonor them. With feelings of despair and isolation, many queer Asian and Pacific American children engage in multiple high-risk behaviors that can compromise, diminish, or destroy them. Such was the case in our own family when our two gay sons, having not been sufficiently acknowledged, validated, protected, and loved as gay children, engaged in a series of hidden, confusing, and complex experiences that contributed to their contracting and dying from illnesses associated with HIV/AIDS. These are things we have learned too late.

If our sons were able to contribute their own chapters to this book, we know that they would have much to teach us. Knowing what our children went through, we imagine that they would say how horrific an experience it was for both of them to grow up gay. Initially, neither knew what it was to be a gay child, and what it meant to have an affinity for others of the same gender. Later, they did not understand why they were subjected to prejudice, discrimination, and hatred because of the nature of their sexual attraction. They would say that they often wanted to learn about themselves and be able to "discuss" themselves with us (parents, relatives, teachers, significant peers, and adults) but most of the time felt that we were inaccessible. They would tell us what it was like to live a "lie" by hiding their true selves, and how so often they felt ashamed of themselves. They would tell us of their feelings of shame and fear because they believed that no one would or could love them because they were gay. They would tell us how "desperate" they were to find the kind of love that would bring them acceptance, respect, and dignity, and how they fell into deep despair when such feelings never materialized.

Our youngest son, Guy, while experiencing all the fear, apprehension, and discomfort associated with having AIDS, became an HIV/AIDS educator during the last two years of his life. We imagine that he would give the following message:

> In order for children growing up "queer" to feel acknowledged, validated, protected, and loved, parents and the adult community must first be willing to listen to queer children. We collectively must do everything possible to make their special world safe, one that will not in any way abandon them, a safe world that not only listens to them, but encourages them to speak out about their fear, confusion, and need for understanding, acceptance, and love. Such opportunities to voice everything about what it means to grow up queer are not only rare but, for most queer children, virtually nonexistent.

The contributors to this book give us all an opportunity not only to better understand the experiences of Asian and Pacific American children growing up queer, but also to validate, honor, and dignify the voices of people who for too long have remained silent. We wish our sons had such an opportunity during the course of their struggles, for if they did, they might still be alive today.

Alexander and Jane Nakatani
Honor Thy Children, Inc.

Alexander and Jane Nakatani are the cofounders and principal administrators of Honor Thy Children, Inc., a nonprofit organization dedicated to promoting the acceptance of human diversity through educational activities that facilitate the understanding and management of human and self-denigration. Since 1994, they have made hundreds of appearances throughout the United States. Their story is chronicled in the book and the video documentary, *Honor Thy Children*. Anyone interested in scheduling Al and Jane Nakatani can do so by contacting <alnakatani@honorthychildren.org>.

Preface

Repeated again and again in our lives are various stories about who we are. We hear these stories in the media, in political debates, in schools, even in our everyday conversations at work, at play, and at home. Some of these stories have become repeated so often in our lives that we have come to think of them as "common sense," as simply the way things are "supposed" to be. But of course, no single story can capture the entirety of who we are. Any one story can offer only a partial understanding of our experiences and identities, and therein lies the problem. When only certain stories become accepted in society, we begin to overlook our complexities, our differences, and the many ways that we exceed our stories. The commonsensical stories begin to define and limit the possibilities of who we are and who we are supposed to be.

Consider, for example, those of us who are identified by ourselves and by others as both Asian/Pacific American and queer. Different communities tell different stories of what it means to be queer and Asian/Pacific American, and while some of these stories can affirm our differences, other stories can be quite oppressive. This should not be surprising. Our stories are based on identities that are themselves problematic. Both "queer" and "Asian/Pacific American" are identifications that were initially imposed on our communities by mainstream U.S. society. Anyone who expressed sexual desires or gender identities in "abnormal" ways were labeled "queer," despite the frequency of intersexed births (that is, babies born neither male nor female), and despite the recognition that same-sex attraction is actually valued in other societies. Anyone who descended from the peoples of Asia and the Pacific islands were labeled "Asian/Pacific American," despite the tremendous diversity among Asian and Pacific Islander cultures, and despite the historical conflicts among Asian and Pacific ethnic groups. Of course, "queer" and "Asian/Pacific American" have recently come to be embraced as political identities that highlight ways in which popular notions of sexual normalcy and racial sameness can be very problematic. But all too often, the categories continue to invoke these homophobic and racist stories.

Mainstream U.S. society tells a range of stories about Asian/Pacific Americans, and these stories often perpetuate stereotypes. Some stories suggest that to be Asian/Pacific American is to be more Asian/Pacific Islander than "American." We are more loyal to some distant "home" than to the United States and are, therefore, a social, political, even economic threat. Some stories identify us all as recently arrived foreigners who cannot speak English well and have difficulty learning "American" culture and values. Some place us in exotic tropical paradises where we exist merely as tourist attractions and objects of desire. Some depict us as a bad minority of refugees who invade a community and drain it of its resources. Some praise us for being a good minority of immigrants—the "model minority"—who works tirelessly, assimilates with little trouble, and enjoys financial success. Not surprisingly, some offer us as proof that the United States is not a racist society and suggest that other "minorities" could also achieve the "American dream" if only they would work as hard as we do.

Mainstream U.S. society also tells many stories of what it means to be queer, a label that encompasses people who are bisexual, lesbian, gay, transgender, intersexed, or are simply questioning their gender or sexuality. As with stories of Asian/Pacific Americans, these stories perpetuate a range of stereotypes. Some stories define same-sex attraction as unnatural, and gender deviation as a problem to be fixed. Some classify nonhetero sex acts as crimes to be persecuted or, at least, sins to be pitied. Some depict queer people as ill, as contagious, and as recruiters, corrupters, or molesters of youth who, free from such exposure, would otherwise grow up heterosexual. Furthermore, some stories suggest that society would be better off if the queers were silenced, excluded, beaten down, and even eliminated.

Of course, within mainstream U.S. society, some communities are telling stories that can help to challenge these stereotypical ones. Asian/Pacific American communities often tell stories that affirm what it means to be Asian/Pacific American. Some stories highlight the cultures, traditions, and heritages of each Asian/Pacific American ethnic group. Some stories help bring us together into a pan-ethnic, politically oriented community by revealing ways in which different ethnic groups confront similar experiences with racism. Some stories honor the contributions that Asian/Pacific Americans have made to U.S. society. Some stories look to earlier times in Asia or the Pacific Islands to find cultural practices and histories that have helped to make us who we are.

Similarly, queer communities often tell stories that affirm what it means to be queer. Some stories suggest that social change cannot happen until society erases the stigma attached to being queer and, perhaps more importantly, rejects the value and the restrictiveness of being "normal." Some stories celebrate different kinds of relationships and redefine commonsensical definitions of the family. Some stories illustrate the variety of paths that have led individuals to come out and embrace queer identities, and to take pride in the contributions queers have made to U.S. society. Some stories refuse to hide our differences or make apologies and instead increase the visibility of queer forms of self-expression, cultural practices, and political movements.

Although the stories told in Asian/Pacific American communities and in queer communities affirm the value of racial and sexual differences with respect to mainstream American society, ironically, these same stories often continue to repeat mainstream stories that oppress these communities. In attempting to challenge one form of oppression (the racism facing Asian/Pacific Americans, the heterosexism facing queers) such stories sometimes unintentionally, and sometimes not, perpetuate other forms of oppression. Asian/Pacific American communities might be helping to affirm our senses of identity and community as Asian/Pacific Americans by defining the family as something of utmost importance in "traditional" Asian cultures. However, the type of family being valued is only that which conforms to conventional, heterosexist notions of family. Being a virtuous Asian/Pacific American often requires getting married, raising children, and carrying on the family name, which means that "real" Asians and Pacific Islanders practice heterosexuality. Queer sexualities are simply not a part of the stories of many Asian/Pacific Americans but are instead often considered particular to white Americans, what some have called a "white disease."

Queer communities also tell stories that operate in contradictory ways, especially when the stories they tell are of queers who primarily are white Americans. Stories of what it means to be queer and what it means to address the needs of queers do not often address cultural and other differences and do not challenge the ways that whiteness is privileged in U.S. society. When queer communities do acknowledge Asian/Pacific Americans, they often reinforce stereotypes. Some queers patronize queer Asian/Pacific Americans because they presume we are needy foreigners or passive model minorities, while others desire queer Asian/Pacific Americans because they perceive us to be exotic. Even the stories that queer researchers tell often represent white American expressions of queer sexualities as normal and those of queer Asian/Pacific Americans that differ as somehow deviant.

We often claim that our Asian/Pacific American and queer communities are places where we can turn for support and to hear alternative and more affirming stories of who we are and who we can be. However, all too often, our communities make it difficult to embrace our identities as both queers and Asian/Pacific Americans. How can we be both when Asian/Pacific Americans are "supposed" to be straight and queers are "supposed" to be white? Invested as we are in fighting oppression, our communities cannot ignore the ironic ways in which stories that challenge one form of oppression simultaneously contribute to others. Such ironies are perhaps not surprising: As with any form of activism, saying who we are and what we are working to change requires simultaneously saying who we are not and what we are not working to change, and these boundaries often marginalize some of the very people we presume to include in our struggles. We need to find ways for Asian/Pacific American activism to challenge heterosexism and embrace all Asian/Pacific Americans, not just straight ones. And we need to find ways for queer activism to challenge racism and embrace all queers, not just white ones.

Fortunately, as more and more activists speak from the margins of our communities, our abilities to recognize and address intersections have increased. In particular, we have heard from more and more queer Asian/Pacific Americans who have taken the initiative to create new and more affirming stories of who we are and what it can mean to be both queer and Asian/Pacific American. They tell stories about our multiple identities and the ways we can experience and challenge multiple forms of oppression. They make it impossible for our communities to ignore the ways in which our activist movements operate in contradictory ways. They bear witness to experiences of growing up, learning about ourselves, forming relationships, and simply living lives that, until now, have been silenced. They show us that, yes, there are queer Asian/Pacific Americans out there, and we are not necessarily what commonsensical stories would have us expect.

But stories by and about queer Asian/Pacific Americans are not always unproblematic. In fact, sometimes, these stories function in exactly the ways I have critiqued the other stories for functioning: They continue to privilege only certain groups in their communities. They claim to be talking about all queer Asian/Pacific Americans, but their stories often focus solely on certain Asian/Pacific American ethnic groups, or certain queer subgroups, or certain genders, socioeconomic classes, body types, and so on. This is perhaps not surprising. East Asian/Pacific Americans have traditionally been privileged in Asian/Pacific American communities and this privilege is often expressed in the stories told by this community, just as gay men and lesbians often have a privileged place in queer communities. Men, the middle and wealthy classes, and the able-bodied or shapely have traditionally been privileged in both communities as well as in mainstream society. What would it mean to tell stories that consciously work against traditional forms of privilege, that refuse to repeat commonsensical notions of who we are as queers and Asian/Pacific Americans and all else with which we identify? What would it mean to tell very different kinds of stories about ourselves? To restory ourselves?

This book tries to do just that. Queer Asian/Pacific Americans who engage in various forms of antioppressive activism have come together to share their autobiographies. We identify with a range of ethnicities, sexual orientations, genders, ages, geographic locations, religions, countries of origin, educational backgrounds, language abilities, and body types. We advocate various perspectives and aim for various goals. We engage in many different forms of activism: Our activisms target queers, Asian/Pacific Americans, queer Asian/Pacific Americans, youth, women, the working poor, families, immigrants, adoptees, Christians, particular ethnic groups, particular age groups, and many other groups. Our activisms operate on school and college campuses, around legislative debates and public referenda, through social-service providers, over the Internet, in art and writing, and by other venues both at the grassroots level and more broadly nationally and internationally. Our activisms address issues of affirmative action, HIV/AIDS education, mental health, school safety, domestic relationships, sexual violence, media representation, community organizing, interracial relations, sweatshop labor, and coalition building. Our activisms work to change legal mandates, religious institutions, educational experiences, corporate practices, cultural traditions, and common knowledges.

Our stories of growing up and engaging in activism help to trouble and complicate commonsensical views of what it means to be queer and Asian/Pacific American, and of what it means to work against multiple forms of oppression. We hope many will use our stories in ways that challenge the oppressive ones mentioned earlier. We hope many will find our stories meaningful in their own lives. We hope many will respond to our stories with new ways of identifying themselves, new ways of building communities, new ways of forming relationships, new ways of thinking about differences in society, and new ways of bringing about social change. We especially hope that youth will feel our stories to be helpful in their own process of restorying themselves.

Our book contributes to the growing literature by, for, and about queer Asian/Pacific Americans committed to social justice. Recently published books include Rakesh Ratti's *A Lotus of Another Color: An Unfolding of the South Asian Gay and Lesbian Experience* (Alyson, 1993); Sharon Lim-Hing's *The Very Inside: An Anthology of Writing by Asian and Pacific Islander Lesbian and Bisexual Women* (Sister Vision Press, 1994); Russell Leong's *Asian American Sexualities: Dimensions of the Gay and Lesbian Experience* (Routledge, 1996); Molly Fumia's *Honor Thy Children: One Family's Journey to Wholeness* (Conari Press, 1997); David Eng and Alice Hom's *Q&A: Queer in Asian America* (Temple University Press, 1998); Quang Bao, Hanya Yanagihara, and Timothy Liu's *Take Out: Queer Writing from Asian Pacific America* (Asian American Writers' Workshop, 2001); David Eng's *Racial Castration: Managing Masculinity in Asian America* (Duke University Press, 2001); and Andrew Matzner's *'O Au No Keia: Voices from Hawai'i's Mahu and Transgender Communities* (Xlibris, 2001).

Of course, our stories are not without their share of problems. Our stories do not tell "all" stories, and there were and are many other stories and parts of stories that could not be included in this one book. Our stories are partial. They are not the final answer to the problems described earlier, and they are just part of the process of affirming who we are and challenging multiple forms of oppression. After all, no book can encapsulate the infinite diversity among queer Asian/Pacific Americans, just as no single story can tell everything about any one author. Stories are *always* partial. They include some things and exclude others. They teach some perspectives and silence others. They support some ideas and critique others. They affect each of us in different ways. Recognizing this partiality requires that we read stories in activist ways. As readers, we must refuse to read these stories as we have traditionally read stories. We cannot read this book and then think that we now know what it means to be queer Asian/Pacific American. We must find ways of reading that complicate what we know, that discomfort how we feel, that trouble how we see ourselves, and that inspire us to act.

As the activists in this book reread and restory their lives, and as they reflect on and share insights from their activisms, they suggest to us what it might mean to read in activist ways. Their stories and the ways they tell their stories have much to teach us. I invite us all to read, to reread, and to be open to the changes they help to make possible in society and in our lives today.

Acknowledgments

A big fabulous *thank you* goes to Dr. John De Cecco and the editors and staff at The Haworth Press for supporting this project and making it possible for us to share our stories through the publication of this book.

Thanks to Eric Collum who was unquestionably generous, insightful, and thorough when helping to clarify the ideas in and strengthen the language and organization of earlier drafts of this book.

Thanks to Bates College, which generously provided a research fund to support this project, and to Clementine Brasier and the student assistants for helping, often at the last minute, with the many and various tasks involved in putting this together.

A special thanks to the many activists whose movements toward social justice—both past and future, both large and small, both visible and unfamiliar—have inspired and continue to inspire us to do the work that we do. Many activists wrote autobiographies that could not be included in this volume, but as more books get published, we can look forward to the time when additional stories will touch our lives.

An Interview
with a High School Activist

Pabitra Benjamin

This chapter is based on an interview I gave in 1999. Because the interviewer asked me to reflect on my experiences as a queer Asian American activist in high school, I thought it would be ideal to use the interview to put together my chapter for this book. I remember thinking, when I first began looking over the original interview transcript, that the whole story just had to be redone. There were many changes that I wanted to make. However, as I started thinking about how change and growth are ongoing processes, I realized that it would be wrong to revamp my story. These words are the thoughts and emotions that I had at the time of the interview. I am still young and have a lot to learn, but what I have recognized through life so far is that change is a fluid flow of development of myself and those around me. My identities combine with my histories to make me who I am, and yet, my identities are only a part of the process of my discovering different ways to work toward revolution. Here, then, is the story I told when I was a senior in high school.

Sophomore year is when I really started identifying myself as queer or bi and associating with that part of the school community. Looking back on it, throughout my childhood, I had always known that I had feelings that differed from the norm, but I never knew what it was because it was never apparent. There wasn't the choice to be gay.

A year earlier, during my first year in high school, one of my mom's friends, who is gay, said, "I think your daughter's gay." My mom said, "No, no, no," and later came up to me and asked me. I answered, "Of course not." But that same year I started making friends with seniors, the "weird" ones who were gay or experimenting. They made me think and question myself. Sophomore year I met more people, and I made friends who were very open about differences. I ended up falling deeply for some females, and that's when I came out. In my junior year I ended up falling for my current girlfriend. I didn't get her until a year later, but I got her!

The hardest thing about being queer is that my mom doesn't know. As in "traditional" Nepali culture, she wants grandchildren and she wants a son-in-law and she wants a "normal" life. If I told her I was gay, it would threaten this dream that she's always had. It's possible that she could respond positively and say, "Great, I knew, I'm glad you told me, you can still have kids and you can adapt." But more likely I think she'd freak out. She would never kick me out, she'd never disown me, but we would have a lot of tension for a while. And eventually she may come about but it's just not something that I'm ready to deal with right now.

I told my dad in the beginning of this year. Nowadays, he doesn't care. My girlfriend sleeps over and he's very comfortable with that, in contrast to my mom who keeps asking why I'm with my girlfriend so often. But my dad wasn't always that comfortable. Early on, we had a long discussion, an hours-long discussion about it. He has always been a very open-minded man and he just said that he would start talking about it more in order to get rid of his own homophobia. As for my mom, my dad and I talked about whether or not we should tell her, and decided not to, at least not yet. My brother knows about it and he's comfortable with it. I had told my brother before I told my father. Actually, my brother kept it a secret for two years, which is amazing because he's a little boy (he's eleven now).

It's interesting that my dad's been so open because of the fact that, or perhaps despite the fact that, for him, fighting homophobia is not a big fight. He once told me, "I don't think it's a fight. It's not as important to me as oppression in third-world countries." But it is! Our lives have been quite different. My dad's American. My birth father died when I was young, so my dad married my mom when I was three or four, and has been my dad since. He's from Chicago, but lived in Nepal half his life, doing his PhD and master's there.

I also have moved around quite a bit. I've lived in four different states, two different countries. As a result, I've had many different types of friends. When I lived in Nepal, my closest friends were from all over the world because I went to an international school. Then I came to Wisconsin, to a place where everybody was just white, and it was hard adjusting. It was difficult trying to find myself when everyone around me was white and when I was not only one of the only students of color, but also one who was able to acknowledge this racial difference. On top of that, there's the fact that I lived a very out lifestyle. Some of the worst memories I have were of trying to fit, to be accepted with all of my identities. If I were in Nepal, it would be even more so the case that I can't be out as gay or bi. In Nepal, our family's not like American Nepalis. They're Nepali Nepali. They're middle class, live in small apartments, and don't speak very much English. Their ideas are very "traditional," so it would be difficult. Similarly, if I lived in a queer community in the United States, I don't know if I'd be accepted as Asian. I wish I could live in a world where I could just be all of it at once.

Changing communities has been the focus of my activism since the beginning of high school. Over the past few years, I've been involved in about twenty-five groups. I led about six of them, and actually started three of them. What prompted my involvement in all these groups was my earlier experience in a group called Bridges. The purpose of Bridges was to unite people, and we worked mostly on racial harmony and racial understanding. We took an approach to racial harmony that did not simply acknowledge that, "Okay, there's a lot of racism," but actually examined racism and brought difficult topics out in the open. After Bridges, in ninth and tenth grades, I continued to involve myself in work that dealt with race relations. More recently, in my junior and senior years, I've been doing work that deals more specifically with sexuality and homophobia.

I think racism and homophobia are part of the same fight. But I know many people don't agree. I see a lot of anger coming from both communities. I hear African Americans or Asian Americans say, "Oh, well, they're gay and they're the ones that reinforce that stereotype of gay people." Similarly, I hear GLBT people say, "Oh wow, they're enforcing the stereotype of us and we don't like that, and they're really mean," as was the case in response to Ron Greer, a black minister who led anti-GLBT efforts in Wisconsin recently. There's just a lot of bitterness. Sometimes different communities of color fight each other rather than joining to fight racism. African Americans and Asian Americans often don't get along here. I think many African

Americans think that Asian Americans are making a lot of money. It's a stereotype that isn't always true, but they sometimes focus on how Asians own the grocery stores and are taking the money of the African-American communities who live nearby. The two groups are forced by society to mix together in ways that end up separating them. I wish there was a way that we could just unite instead of having to fight about little differences.

Since my first year in high school, one of my main goals has been to have some sort of day when everybody could get together to celebrate our differences and the diversity among us. Last year, we started a Diversity Day where we had booths set up by different student groups. This year, we had three days of Diversity Days. The first day we had speakers and performances. The second day we had panels all day long. The third day we had a potluck. The events were small but very effective. My goal over these past two years was to keep it continuing and to involve more of the school and not just a few classes in the celebration. This year, out of a population of 2,000 students, at least 500 or 600 took part. That was one of my largest accomplishments.

Another big accomplishment was my school's GSA. In my junior year, I helped start a gay-straight alliance with three senior friends. This year, since all three friends had graduated, I took over the leadership of the GSA, and we became one of the largest clubs at my high school. We had about thirty members, with around fifteen people coming to the weekly meetings. Most of them were straight, though we never asked about anyone's sexual orientation, especially since some had not yet decided. The group provided both a supportive space and a means for activism. For example, at the beginning of the year, we decided that one of our main goals would be to stop students from using the word "gay" as a form of verbal bashing. It was extremely commonplace to hear "That's so gay" or "He's such a fag." By the end of the year, the use of such language had noticeably decreased. We even heard people whom we previously thought to be homophobic say things like, "You know what, I don't like the use of that language." It was exciting to think that, by going out and standing strong, we started that. We were on a mission, and through personal contacts, got more and more people to help spread that knowledge.

This is one of the most important areas where teachers need to do more. They need to acknowledge that gay-bashing happens, that little things like name-calling are part of a bigger circle of homophobia that permeates schools. If teachers heard the word "nigger," they would automatically jump, but if they hear the word "gay," they often let it go instead of stopping and saying, "You know, let's talk about this." And I don't mean that teachers should merely say, "No, that's wrong, don't use that word." They need to stop class and have a discussion. It might take only five minutes, but they need to say, "Let's talk about this."

In fact, teachers need to be prepared to talk about any sort of subject that comes up—sexism, racism, homophobia, anything. I think that that is the most important thing for which teachers need preparation. The leaders of the local school board recently called me. They're planning a workshop for the entire school board on how to deal with GLBTQ students. I'm going to be involved in that workshop. More opportunities are needed to take steps like that to educate members of the school board who can then educate teachers. Teachers and students need to talk. There needs to be a day on which teachers could have an in-service workshop, not about graduation tests, but about what it's like for GLBTQ high school students. That would be a major help.

There was a time when I was sitting on a school lawn with my girlfriend, just sitting there like two friends, tickling, whatever. All of a sudden this guy comes up to her and says, "Why don't you just stop that 'cause that's nasty. I mean you guys just look . . ." And I said, "What? You know what, if you could ask a little bit nicer, I would stop, even though I don't know what I'm doing wrong." We got in this huge fight and he said, "Come on, bitch, come hit me." And I said, "What are you talking about?" There were around seventeen or eighteen people out there. I asked, "Who here thinks this guy is wrong?" Everybody raised their hands, including his friends. It may have been wrong for me to isolate him, but that's the way I do things; I'm very blunt. I wanted him to know that he was wrong.

This is the kind of environment that exists in schools. And what happens in school affects our experiences elsewhere because people gossip and talk. Gay couples can be conversation topics for many other people. My girlfriend's mom is a teacher, and the news that we were going out had spread from a far-west-side high school to a far-east-side elementary school. Thankfully, she already knew. But we were teachers' gossip for a while. And that's probably the hardest part of high school life. I don't ever know what people are really thinking. I'm not saying that people ever understand who they are but high school can be a pretty confusing time without this added problem. The secrecy often surrounding homophobia impacts all of our lives.

Fortunately, my family upbringing prepared me to live with independence and self-confidence. My family and I have lived all sorts of lifestyles. We have traveled and lived in many places because my dad gets jobs here and gets fired there. With all these changes, my parents are used to giving me lots of freedom. It's as if they say, "Just go on, do whatever you want. We're not going to keep an eye out every minute." They trust me. They didn't know about all of my extracurricular activities until I started winning awards. Even now, they don't know about half of what I do, but they know I do things and are okay with that. If I come home at three in the morning, they do ask, "Why are you late?" but if I simply say, "I was with a friend doing this," they trust me. That trust and ability to just go and do whatever I wanted to do helped me become an activist. It helped me see the kind of changes I wanted to make. It did not lead to what parents often fear, namely, that "Oh, if I give my kids freedom, they're going to go and do drugs and everything, go get in trouble." Yes, I've done drugs and things like that, but that's been a part of my growing-up experiences. And being allowed to try different things is important.

I think the most important advice I can give to anybody is what I said about my parents: Parents need to let their children go. Not all kids will do good things. But parents need to accept the ways their children are different, be they GLBT or simply choosing to do some things and not following the paths of others. Parents need to talk to their kids, know how to help them, and even define some boundaries together, but let them be on their own. I can't give advice about how to stop racism or how to stop homophobia, but I can say that a lot more youths are coming out these days. If you have a friend whose child is GLBT, be willing to go up to that child or your friend, or anyone, and just talk to them about it. Talk to your friends about how it's okay.

2

Curry Potatoes and Rainbow Banners

Nur-e-alam S. Chisty

Too often my identity has been an absence, a list of things I am not or a list of the things I should not be. I was the wrong one: wrong lips, wrong nose, wrong self. As a child I would go to sleep wishing that when I awoke I would be white. I am no longer a child, but that child has not died. And so I write.

Reginald Shepherd,
"On Not Being White"

The brown paper bag smelled of the slightly over-cooked spicy Indian potatoes that my mother had prepared for my first day at "the American school" in Long Island, New York. While it would later draw unwelcome attention, at the moment the odor was strangely mesmerizing. My stomach growled at the thought of savoring this Indian specialty. As a new immigrant to the United States, my only exposure to the English language in Dhaka, Bangladesh, my native country, was from battered television and VCR manuals. Nonetheless, I was able to comprehend clearly the word "lunch" as soon as it was announced to the class.

With little patience, I reached for my lunch bag, allowing the source of the piquant smell to come closer to my taste buds. As always, my mother had organized the bag with meticulous care, with a Hi-C drink wrapped neatly in a collection of florid Bounty paper towels, and a small container of roughly ten spicy curry potatoes. I quickly grabbed my plastic fork to begin enjoying this delicacy. "Delicious," I thought, after I took my long-awaited first bite. As I eagerly prepared to take the next bite, this moment of appreciation and utter contentment was crudely interrupted.

"Curry-smelling Gandhi man, what the fuck," a white boy yelled as he subsequently pinched his nose and ran away, making sure to leave me with his facial expression of utter disgust. While I failed to understand any of his words except "Gandhi," his actions were enough to convey his message clearly.

I threw out my lunch unfinished that day, returning home famished, degraded, and confused. When my mother questioned me on my melancholy tone of voice, I answered with an explanation of the day's events. I awaited a sympathetic hug. Actually, on that day, I would have settled for an encouraging pat on the back. Instead, all I received was a powerful misunderstanding.

"Well, Gandhi was a great man darling, so the next time they say it, you say 'thank you,' okay?"

This event was a landmark in my life, giving me a first taste of the pervasive racist mentality of U.S. society. In addition, it taught me that my parents did not and perhaps would never understand or empathize with my struggles in constructing an Asian American identity. Today, reflecting on these hateful memories allows me to empower myself and even entertain thoughts of punching those individuals who made such racist remarks to me. However, at the age of ten, I directed my feelings of abhorrence toward myself.

I vividly remember returning home each day from school, having delved deeper into a depression caused by self-hatred. My understanding of race in elementary school mainly consisted of two closely related elements: a deeply embedded sentiment of internalized racism, and a desire to wake up one morning as a white male. I can remember times when my elementary school classmates labeled me as the token ugly, rancid, and illiterate immigrant. Little did I realize how much of this ostracism I had internalized and used to construct my own identity as a self-hating loner! To evade the everyday criticism of my odorous clothes and my indecipherable accent, I had transformed myself into a subservient, quiet, and hard-working adolescent, a haunting replica of the stereotypical Asian American male student. My parents reinforced this identity by stressing how good (and compliant) work ethics and academic success would allow for more upward social mobility.

Even though my parents' urging to fit in was intended to be a form of encouragement, it contributed to my loss of a clear cultural identity. In junior high school, I became increasingly reluctant to comply with my parents' demands to maintain strong ties with "our" culture. My ties to South Asian cultures became less passionate, even while people in school and larger society made it difficult for Asians to feel a part of U.S. society and to identify as "American." In the hopes of becoming more accepted by the popular white students, I immersed myself in pop culture, trying desperately to like MTV and Hollywood movies. What resulted was a true convolution of identities. I was seen as "Asian," which I didn't want to be; I wanted to be "American," which I was learning I could never really be. To which culture, then, did I belong? Society seemed to be teaching new generations of U.S.-born South Asians to adopt identities that are conducive to the demands of both cultures. Yet, my task of being both "American" and "Asian" seemed impossible. "American" ideals were unwelcome at my home, while a staunchly European-centered curriculum at school left little room for a discussion, much less an understanding, of Asian cultures and identities.

Of course, race was not the only problem. Also significantly shaping my identity construction while in school was my sexual orientation. During my adolescence, I covertly and disgustedly admitted to myself my feelings of same-sex attraction. Given that discussions on queer sexuality were and still are virtually nonexistent in contemporary Asian cultures, I came to acknowledge my sexual orientation only late in junior high school when I asked a friend about the true meaning of the overused word "faggot." Significantly, although I failed to come out with pride during my schooling, I was nonetheless taunted for my stereotypically "homosexual behavior." Fearing rejection, especially having witnessed quotidian homophobia in both my Asian and my "American" communities, I felt once again left to cope with my confusion alone. I remember thinking that I was the only queer male of color living in this world.

Although I did try to construct my racial and sexual identities separately, I found it increasingly difficult to think about my sexuality without thinking about my race. The reason behind that is best explained in the work of Reginald Shepherd (1986), the first gay black author I ever encountered:

> My feelings about men are too entangled with my feelings about white men, and my feelings about white men too entangled with my feelings about white people and about black people, especially black men. . . . How to determine how much is racial and

how much is sexual when the two are so entwined that they are, in practice, identical? ("On Not Being White." In Joseph Beam [Ed.], *In the Life: A Black Gay Anthology,* p. 52)

The more I entertained fantasized thoughts about the white males in my school, the more I grew to hate my racial background. I grew to dehumanize myself and humanize only whites, perceiving them to be the only race capable of looking beautiful and accomplishing great things.

A significant portion of this self-disgust resulted from the absence of constructive discussions about race and sexual orientation in my educational endeavors. For example, throughout most of my schooling experiences, any constructive dialogue on homosexuality seemed to be strictly forbidden, and rarely was the use of such pejorative terms as "faggot" or "sissy" reprimanded in classrooms. This absence intensified my feelings of self-hatred until I got hold of such literature as that by Reginald Shepherd, which helped to normalize my identities.

Undoubtedly, tremendous negativity had overshadowed my youth as a result of my own internalized racism and homophobia as well as the discriminations that permeated society. However, a somewhat positive aspect of my quasi-tragic adolescent experience is my emergence as an academically successful student. For example, I remember, after becoming proficient in English, regularly receiving compliments from my teachers on my writing and speaking abilities. Being a member of an "outgroup" in a racially homogenous high school deterred me from trying to relate to other students and have an active social life, and instead, I dedicated tremendous time and energy to academic achievment. As I mentioned earlier, society may have stereotyped Asian Americans as submissive and subordinate, but it also expected from Asian Americans an ethic of hard work and academic success, and I internalized and conformed to these ideals.

Of course, once I learned to "succeed" in academics, I mistakenly began to correlate my success with my race. A close Asian American friend sparked this when he once said, "Of course we're smart, dude; we're Asian." As this was one of the first positive associations I had made with my race, I quickly jumped on the idea that academic success could compensate for the "sinful" aspects of my racial and sexual identities. Through academic achievement, I had hoped to construct a facade that would divert attention from the two identities that otherwise invited degradation. My success in high school would not and did not bring an end to the discrimination I faced on a regular basis. However, it did help me regain the sense of self-worth that I had lost on that first day in the "American" school.

I ended my K-12 schooling naively, still unable to acknowledge the deeply rooted effects of my race and sexual orientation on my identity construction. In fact, it was not until my arrival at Vassar College that I would learn about the complexities of oppression and the imperfections of U.S. society. Only through my college experiences have I learned how to unravel the implications of what was taught and, more important, not taught to me during my school years.

Although I may occasionally reflect on my adolescence with some degree of cynicism, I have now learned to redirect these feelings of anger to fuel my struggles for equality. In college, I have been afforded opportunities to participate actively in such student organizations as the Asian Students' Alliance (ASA) and the Queer Coalition. I remember sighing with relief when I learned that there were other queers of color in this world and that the term "Asian activist" was not just another oxymoron!

However, even in these contexts, I initially found myself questioning whether I truly belonged to either campus organization. While I enthusiastically devoted my energy to both, rarely did I feel my identities as a person of color and a queer person matter simultaneously. For instance, while ASA members readily discussed issues of race during meetings, rarely was the dialogue inclusive of the pervasive racism in queer communities. I began questioning why I had to leave my queerness at the door upon entering any ASA meeting, and similarly, why I had to mask my color when engaging in a dialogue about and with LGBTQ people. Thankfully, an increased knowledge of outside resources allowed me to seek out queers-of-color organizations around my area, which have become spaces for my identities to coexist. And I have since found many benefits bringing my two campus groups to work together.

In surrounding myself with queers, people of color, and queers of color, I have come to construct a niche of individuals who are not necessarily all of the same sexual orientation and race, but who share with me a similar passion in life to teach and make a difference. I have learned that the essence of activism is not only fighting for the causes that affect me, but also building a community of people who desire to fight for causes that affect others as well as themselves.

Nowadays, whether it is at a gay pride parade where I proudly hold a banner for the South Asian Lesbian and Gay Association (SALGA) of New York, at a Black Students' Union event where I show my support for other people-of-color organizations on my campus, or simply in any classroom where I learn or unlearn with my fellow undergraduates, I feel obligated to voice my opinions and remind those who have forgotten that hatred exists. All in all, my goal is to convey to my peers that I am willing to fight for their cause, and all I ask in return is that they walk beside me as I fight for mine. Practicality and my values sometimes forbid me from fighting for every oppressed group and reaching every individual, and I have come to understand my limitations and work within them. Nonetheless, I occasionally allow optimism to fuel my dreams of changing the world.

As I conclude, it is important to understand that this story is merely a portion of the overall events that have led me to construct my identities. Over the years, I have come to accept race and sexuality as unequivocal elements of my everyday life. I no longer see these aspects of my identity as means for my "damnation." Rather, I see them as fueling my vision of using education to rid society of ignorance.

3

We Are Not Gay

Lance Collins

At some point early in life, I was able to understand various desires I had and how to satisfy them discreetly. Disorganized thoughts and feelings were all they were. Even up until high school, I didn't really organize my identity around my desires and my sexual actions. But then something happened: I was identified by others and located onto the hetero/homo map of desire. Suddenly, all that made me me was somehow related to how my desires were organized by the dominant hetero/homo way of knowing. Identity was like a costume—if I accepted it and wore it, I supposedly could articulate every emotion, desire, and thought through it for a more satisfying life. If I recognized myself within this matrix of understanding, I would be empowered.

Of course, this false sense of empowerment only worked for most of my teenage years. Before I turned sixteen, I had finished high school and started college. I became involved in county politics, fighting for those good-natured colonial things every budding liberal should, such as environmental issues, free-speech issues, and of course, "gay" issues. I also became the president of the college student body. However, both college class work and outside discovery led me to question the epistemic foundations (the foundations of knowledge) on which my actions were based.

I found that, being sixteen in college on an island with few people, I experienced a lot of loneliness. All of my friends had left Maui for college and I didn't make any real friends at school. I felt very empty and used politics as a refuge. I would try to think of everything in terms of politics. However, my new, liberating ideas only made me see the guards patrolling the high-security prison within which we were all contained.

I graduated from Maui Community College and left Maui for the University of Hawai'i at Manoa on O'ahu. I lived in an on-campus apartment and my parents had shipped my mom's car over to O'ahu. For many seventeen-year-old college juniors, a car and apartment with no parental supervision might be a dream made in heaven. However, as it happened, I was even more lonely. When on Maui, I still had my family and my home; on O'ahu, I had no one. I dug myself into my studies for about three weeks, and, like all of school, found it boring. I did make friends with a young Korean/black daughter of a military family. She was interested in the same "identity" stuff I was and so we would hang out all the time.

More significantly, I also began a few intimate friendships/relationships with other Asian/Pacific Islander guys who identified as straight. Based on our talks and experiences, there was little question that either they misidentified themselves or that the identifying framework was wrong. From what I gathered by listening to gay activists for some time, the identifying framework would suggest that they were gay but closeted. However, my intuition told me that these guys weren't closeted so much as they didn't constitute their identity based on their sexual acts, and would instead let the heterosexism of the dominating knowledge base misidentify them. At the time, I felt that having an intimate relationship (as friends or whatever) required me to be open to however they self-identified and try to judge as little as possible. When I would recollect this to gay activists later, they would respond with anger toward me in my refusal to identify these guys as gay—or at least bisexual. These relationships and the reaction of others to my participation in them would eventually shape both my activism and my way of knowing.

"Gay" activists affected me in other ways as well. The public referendum to give the state legislature the power to ban same-sex marriage surfaced in Hawai'i in the fall of my senior year in college, the same year that I ran for the Maui-residency, neighbor-island seat on the state Board of Education. To support and defeat the referendum, the Mormon Church/Christian Coalition and the Human Rights Campaign (respectively) penetrated Hawai'i and fought a multimillion-dollar media war against each other. Since I was finishing my degree on O'ahu and my campaign took me to all the other islands anyway, I decided to help the pro-marriage Protect Our Constitution (Human Rights Campaign) side of the media battle.

I noticed immediately that, with the exception of the token Hawaiian or local Asian person here and there, the campaign was run by white people from the continent. They didn't understand local Asian settler culture, Hawaiian culture, or the ambiguous cultural flows and tensions between those two and the white American culture. When critiqued by nobodies like me, they would say that we didn't know because we didn't have experience. Of course, for those three of you who don't know, Hawai'i voted 70 percent to 30 percent to give the state legislature the power to ban same-sex marriage. I lost 44,000 to 48,000 for the Board seat—and by then had shed my liberal philosophy for a radical left one.

There was one ad type that was most unsettling of all the ads, a type used by both sides: the kind stating that there was a connection between the Hawaiian struggle for self-determination and same-sex marriage. Eventually I'd come to figure out that what was most uncomfortable about the ads was the fact that white men and women were coming from the continental United States to Hawai'i to try to persuade voters that voting yes or no was voting for Hawaiian cultural preservation.

The "gay" community appropriates Hawaiian culture all the time. During the first year of its existence, *DaKine* magazine—a local, gay, monthly periodical owned by a white European settler—featured Native-looking men on the front cover of ten of the twelve issues. This first year included the February issue in which preschool-aged Native boys with gym-bunny bodies held hands coming out of the "bush."

These insights prompted me to notice fascism in many places. I turned my life upside down only to find that nothing had a natural moral quality to it. Good and bad existed to reinforce different structures and relations of power. "Straight is good." "Gay is bad." "Out is good." "Closeted is bad." "Asian is good." "White is bad." Different social and cultural dynamics were at work determining what is good and what is bad and compelling us to abide by these ideas. These dynamics even color our identities.

Reading Frantz Fanon and others, I have come to realize many ways in which colonialism has operated among my peoples and the native Hawaiians. Drawing on a childhood marked by cultural influences from the Philippines, Latvia, and white America, I started to engage in personalized discussions on colonialism and Hawaiian sovereignty. I began to explain to others that my identity was not "gay," and that the category was an insidious colonial weapon used to kill the souls of the colonized. My desire hadn't changed much, but the way I organized it and how it organized itself had.

I'll illustrate with a story: The summer after I received my bachelor's degree, I became involved with a social group that was funded by the Department of Health through a local AIDS service provider. Although I made some friends in the group, I found my interest in the group becoming more political as I noticed that although the provider was funded to serve youth most at risk, all events were held in a more affluent area of urban Honolulu.

As it turned out, white and Asian settlers were statistically overrepresented in the geographic area where the group held its social events. Hawaiians, Filipinos, and others were dramatically underrepresented. This is institutional racism. I did some research to make sure I had evidence from the Public Health discipline to back me and I presented my case to the group that oversaw the funded projects, which included staff members in the project. After I summarized my main points, the staff members of the AIDS organization immediately began attacking me personally. The first attack against me was that I had no right to speak to the issue of racism because I looked white. I couldn't say anything. I was shocked. And hurt.

I felt like I had given a very well-thought-out argument and had spoken because my people and Hawai'i's indigenous people were being marginalized. After an hour, the facilitator/chair of the group thanked me for coming. Leaving, I realized that when a group of twelve middle-aged gay men (white and of color) attack a nineteen-year-old boy of color for talking about racism and colonialism, something is very wrong. As I continued to speak out, similar events kept occurring with more frequency.

Colonialism is not merely a moral issue. Colonialism is an epistemic issue. Colonialism is a process in which a foreign way of knowing supplants a Native way of knowing. At different times and different places, this supplantation takes place within the spirit of the Native and by eliminating the Native.

Although I constantly reflect on what colonialism is and my relation to colonialism, a compromise with colonialism is never possible. Colonialism must under all circumstances be openly discredited. Not that our own passions and shortcomings can be glossed over. The struggle against colonialism can never be a blow-for-blow fight, since in the end, we can get caught up in the hatred and passion. We must make progress toward what is good based on our own ways of knowing. We need our own ways to understand our desires, our identities, our communities.

I found that "gay" communities are always and already contributing to maintaining and reinforcing colonialism. "Gay" identity is a European/American invention. With this understanding, everything that gay communities do has colonialist elements. It isn't hard to see that gay communities take over the bodies and histories of Natives, just as missionaries/white American businessmen did their land. In order to free the land, the colonial matrix of understanding must be unbolted from the land and challenged. Likewise, in order to free our bodies, we can no longer see our bodies and selves in terms of the colonial matrix of understanding. "Gay" is a colonial remnant and is a function of a colonial reality.

When I discuss this issue within "gay community" contexts, I am easily dismissed as being a Hawaiian radical—although I am not Hawaiian—or as putting ethnic relations over the fight for gay communities. This, of course, shows another characteristic of gay communities—their dominant ethnic group-ness. In Hawai'i, fighting for "only" gay rights is a white/Asian settler tendency. To understand colonialism and racism as separate political questions from heterosexism, one must believe that being gay is naturally being part of the dominant ethnic group(s).

So now I sit with my desires. I try not to organize them too much—or at least not in colonial ways. My politics are very conscious of the epistemological battles in every action. I am silent in certain ways and make discussion in other ways, hoping that colonialism will no longer be disseminated through sex and our understanding of it.

The most liberating feeling is one that arises when departing from colonialist identities and colonial identity formation. Without the colonial identity, there is no false safety net. There is no false assumption that other people are necessarily participating in a common existence. Without that notion, the ethical reasoning behind violently appropriating the space of other people becomes impossible. We are allowed to be who we are or who we are to become. We can allow ourselves to be vulnerable to others.

– 4 –

Fragmented Entries, Multiple Selves: In Search of a Place to Call Home

Roland Sintos Coloma

Part I

Until I came to the United States I had never considered myself or even been called an Asian American or Pacific Islander. Prior to my family's "visit" to the United States in December 1985, a month after I turned thirteen, I did not spend a lot of time wondering who and what I was. I knew that my father had Spanish blood in him, especially since my grandfather looked mestizo. My grandmother from my mother's side claimed Chinese ancestry. Nonetheless it seemed very simple: I was born in the Philippines; therefore I was Filipino.

My family and I had a relatively comfortable life in the Philippines. Both parents held managerial civil-service positions in government agencies. My two oldest siblings were enrolled in prestigious universities, my other sister finished high school ahead of time, and I had begun my first year in a college preparatory high school. But after thirteen years of waiting for the U.S. Embassy to process and approve our immigration applications (because my aunt, who had been living in the United States since the mid-1960s, was the one who petitioned for my mom and my family, our application fell into the "fifth preference" category, which had very low priority and took longer to process), we finally got our papers and decided to take a well-deserved vacation to the United States. I yearned to experience the "white Christmas" with the snow-covered pine trees and hills that I had seen on the covers of greeting cards. I was finally going to eat all the apples and chocolates that I wanted and would not have to wait to open the *balikbayan* boxes that our relatives sent us during the holiday seasons. My dreams were about to come true.

Our stay in the United States was supposed to be temporary, but in early 1986, the Philippines began to undergo a dramatic social and political revolution. Concerned for our safety, my parents decided that the entire family would stay with our aunt and her family in San Jose, California, until it was safe to go back. That was more than fifteen years ago, and I still have not returned to the Philippines. Over the years, I have seen more of the United States than of the country I used to consider "home." In 1987, the white Christmas I yearned for became a reality when my family and I visited my dad's sisters in Chicago. In 1990, I experienced desert heat when I started my first year at college in southern California. In 1994, I touched the Statue of Liberty during a memorable East Coast trip with my dad. Soon after, I took a two-week road trip around the Great Lakes, and then headed to the South to learn community organizing. Now, many years after I left the Philippines, I write about these recollections in a modest apartment in Ohio, alone, away from my family, undergoing my own social and political revolution.

Growing up in the Bay Area of northern California from the mid- to late 1980s was difficult for me. As the youngest child in a working-class, immigrant, devoutly Catholic, Filipino home, I was expected to defer to my parents and older siblings, to be diligent with my chores and studies, to work part time after school and on weekends, and to pursue activities that contributed positively and financially to my family. As the only one educated in a U.S. high school, I was also perceived by my family as someone who would excel academically and eventually obtain a professional job and assimilate into mainstream society. For my parents, our family survival in the United States was top priority, so they encouraged me to participate and do well in school and the extracurricular activities that would put me in contact with more white, middle-class teenagers, many of whom seemed not to have the same kinds of pressures and responsibilities that I had. The dichotomous and confusing roles of obediently following my filial duties as the youngest son in an Asian American and Pacific Islander family and of constantly transforming myself to assimilate into predominantly white, middle-class institutions were challenging.

My parents' administrative backgrounds and my siblings' college education from the Philippines mattered little in the United States. My father and brother worked in the assembly lines of electronics factories. My mother became a nurse's aide in a convalescent hospital, and my two sisters flipped burgers in fast-food chains. The cramped two-bedroom apartment where the living room couch served as my bed was dramatically different than the well-furnished homes I had been invited to for sumptuous dinners in the Philippines. My parents and siblings, their Filipino accents and fresh-off-the-boat (FOB) clothing, and the smell of homemade Filipino food, especially *bagoong,* elicited in me feelings of shame. I was too embarrassed at that time to bring friends home or bring my family to school. What would my classmates, teachers, and other parents think of them? Of me?

I entered junior high—a bastion of conformity and peer pressure—a month after we arrived in the United States. It was difficult to show up with the "wrong" haircut and unfashionable clothes. What I thought was the latest style in the Philippines did not mirror the "cooler" U.S. version. It was condescending to be placed in a remedial math course after I had already finished algebra in the Philippines, or to be placed in an ESL class without taking an English-proficiency exam. I would like to think that the school administrators did not base their placement decisions on my parents' clothing and accent when they registered me for school, or on my school registration card where I marked U.S. noncitizen and Asian American and Pacific Islander under ethnicity, checked English as a nonprimary or nonhome language, and copied my alien registration number from my green card. It was difficult to pick up the slang and common expressions and mimic the "valley" accent in order to be understood. It was difficult to seek the approval and company of the popular kids in school, and, in order to fit in, to change into somebody my family could no longer recognize. The message was loud and clear to me: Assimilating in the United States meant denying my family, my culture, my language, myself.

Part II

I graduated from high school at the age of seventeen. Although my parents wanted me to go back to the Philippines, I envied my classmates who were applying to universities here in the United States. Without my parents' consent or family guidance, I bravely applied to universities, even to a couple of elite ones, and was fortunately accepted into them. I eventually decided to matriculate into a southern

California university that provided the most generous financial aid package and was close enough to, yet far enough away from, my family. I was the only one from my high school to attend this university. I saw it as an opportunity for another fresh start.

The first week of school coincided with fraternity rush. My preconceived image of college life was one in which mostly white fraternities and sororities were the center of social activities. My undergraduate campus seemed no different. I hesitantly decided to rush, afraid that I would not fit their standards. After four grueling nights of countless introductions, themed events, and self-marketing, I received an offer to join my first choice, one of the most sought-after Greek houses on campus. I wanted to join a group of men who were involved in student activities and athletics, promoted leadership and academic values, and ensured popularity and easy access to various functions. I wanted to be somebody and yearned to belong. Of course I accepted their offer.

I thought that joining a fraternity would resolve my predicament in socializing with, relating to, or being in the company of men. I had wondered if this difficulty was due to my emotionally aloof father and brother, or my generously affectionate mother and sisters. Regardless of my speculations, I was more drawn to socializing with women because I was able to share emotionally when with them. I felt that I could be vulnerable and tender with my female friends without risking ridicule and attacks on my masculinity. My women friends valued and encouraged care and compassion. I admired their strength, firm conviction, and direct communication skills. I relied on them for emotional and physical support. Yet I felt confused. I often asked myself, "Am I supposed to be acting and feeling this way?" In contrast, my male friends tended to focus on terse communication, fierce physical competition, and rigid definitions of power, pride, and reputation. There always seemed to be an invisible wall encouraging emotional and physical distance between and among men. My male and female friends gave me conflicting lessons about how men can and should interact with one another.

My schooling in the Philippines had taught me additional lessons. When my family moved to Manila in order to prepare for our departure to the United States, I attended for a year and a half an all-boys' Catholic school that had a small yet visible group of *baklas* who were perceived as stereotypically effeminate. Maybe due to my "less masculine" manners and characteristics, I became an additional recruit to the crew. These older students taught me how to play a killer game of volleyball, tutored me in math and science, showed me the latest fads in magazines, and mentored me in the ways of attracting men. I was a quick learner! Within a year, I played volleyball religiously, ranked first academically in my class, turned into a trendy city boy, and drew the interest of an ROTC officer. I learned to clearly demarcate my interactions with straight male friends and classmates from my interactions with *baklas*. Lines were drawn, and my worlds separated. I even learned to lead separate home and school lives, a conscientious practice that carried over in the United States. I told my family what they needed and wanted to hear. Even friends knew only certain parts of me.

Yet, I could not have been a *bakla*. Although close friendships ensued between my *bakla* friends and me, their romantic interests differed from mine. They tended to focus exclusively on so-called "real" or macho men, and desired to be like women. They yearned for relationships somewhat similar to heterosexual relationships and readily assumed the stereotypical role of nurturing, understanding women. In the Philippines, *baklas* were generally seen in the artistic and fashion careers of couture designers and beauty salon owners, and appeared in movies and television sitcoms primarily as flamboyant comic relief. Some were known to have endured physically and emotionally abusive relations with men. Some had partners who identified as heterosexual, who married women and raised their own families while maintaining "homosexual" affairs for financial reasons. I did not see myself leading this life of the stereotypical *bakla*. *Silahis* also would not have been an appropriate label for me since it usually referred to married men who engage in sexual behavior with other "heterosexual" men. Behavior should not be the determining factor in sexual identification. If that were the case, I would have labeled and actually did label myself "straight" as I had had sex only with women until after my undergraduate years. Calling myself heterosexual would be inappropriate since such a label negates my inherent attraction to people's overall aura and being, regardless of their gender, sex, or sexual orientation.

I never fully understood what bisexuality meant until I came across the anthology, *Bi Any Other Name,* in college. It explained that identifying as bisexual reflects a person's potential for emotional, romantic, and/or physical involvement with another person, regardless of gender, in either reality or fantasy (and does not reflect a person's involvement with people of different genders simultaneously). After reading the personal anecdotes in the anthology and stories and essays in other books, I felt relieved and affirmed. I finally found a term for my unspoken and hidden desires, and a group of people with whom I could relate and whose experiences validated my own. Since identity had nothing to do with sexual behavior or history, I came out to myself as a bisexual prior to having sex with a man. Perhaps I had always been a bisexual; I just never knew the "correct" term. Unfortunately I could not share this self-revelation and either my joy or my struggle with anyone. I was not ready to come out publicly.

Joining a fraternity and conforming my behavior, appearance, and language to the dominant majority were my strategies of straightening up and e-race-ing whatever made me different. My typical attire consisted of a tucked-in polo shirt, a khaki pair of pants or shorts with a woven leather belt, and a fraternity sweatshirt tied around the waist. I frequently ate my meals in the commons dining hall where a distinct Greek section was boisterous with laughter and activities. I made sure to assume leadership positions in my pledge class and fraternity chapter. I wrote an exemplary report that garnered our international headquarters' highest recognition, and I received the coveted Greek Service Award for my campus leadership and involvement. I felt invaluable and respected in my chapter. Nevertheless, I remained marked. In fraternity pictures and gatherings, I was one of the few people of color, brown-ing the almost lily-white scene. I choreographed our talent show by teaching my fraternity brothers and sorority partners how to "vogue" à la Madonna. I helped with our Greek pyramid competition routine by drawing on my cheerleading experience. No wonder there were incessant rumors and questions about my sexuality.

Ironically, my increased participation in Greek life paralleled my actively growing militancy with campus social-justice groups. I lobbied for additional funding for ethnic student services, advocated for an Asian American Studies program and Vietnamese and Tagalog language courses, and was arrested during a sit-in that addressed institutionalized racism. I learned indispensable lessons from and developed meaningful friendships with older student activists, a few of whom were Asian American and Pacific Islander queer men and queer-positive women. These Asian American and Pacific Islander queer and queer-positive radicals raised my critical consciousness; they represented a strong political voice articulating the concerns of Asian American and Pacific Islander students and other communities of color. This collective managed to infiltrate campus politics and shape the political climate. They became editors and writers of various campus publications, developed strategies for an Asian American and Pacific Islander political action group, and founded a feminist support group. They engaged me in direct action, challenged my assumptions, called me on my shortcomings, and supported my identity development. In addition, these mentors and comrades were a source of encouragement and confidence as I ventured into the more visible positions of coordinating a statewide student network, giving the commencement address, and speaking at community functions. My involvement in campus leadership and community organizing provided me an education beyond the offerings of the four-walled classrooms. It also profoundly shaped my racial and sexual identities.

Part III

I decided to come out publicly as bisexual after I graduated and began working as a student services staff member at my alma mater. I had become financially and professionally secure. I knew I would have the support of my "family" of friends in southern California. By this time, with the exception of holiday and summer visits, I had been away from my biological family for four years. Within a two-year period, I disclosed my sexual orientation to close friends and co-workers, to a few of my fraternity brothers, and slowly to each member of my family. The reactions that I received varied. Some of my friends had suspected that I was not straight prior to my revelation, but had assumed that I was gay, despite that I had been sexually involved exclusively with women in high school and college. One friend commented that I should only date other bisexuals so that it would not be confusing or threatening to gay men and straight women. My co-workers were relatively understanding, and one candidly offered to set me up on dates with other men. My little brother in the fraternity said that my sexuality made no difference in our close relationship, and we continued to exchange warm, platonic hugs when we met. One of my pledge brothers even e-mailed me to commend my honesty and hoped that I continued to be involved with the fraternity.

Surprisingly, my family was supportive, although my parents were concerned about my health status and partner choice as well as the negative social and professional consequences. Initially, they hypothesized that my conscious departure from Catholicism, my infrequent church attendance, and the geographical distance between me and my family contributed to my "confusion." They thought that I went astray because the church and family no longer guided me. My parents also wondered if the way they raised me contributed to this "phase." But after I sat down to talk to them, they assured me that, although they might not necessarily celebrate my bisexuality, they would always love me and be supportive of my choices, relationships, and happiness. I knew I was one of the few fortunate ones. Some of my bisexual, transgender, lesbian, and gay friends had related disastrous coming-out stories to me. A few chose not to reveal their sexual and gender orientations to their family, fearing negative consequences. Since my coming out, I have witnessed my family's gradual ease over the issue of (nonhetero) sexuality. Topics such as gays in the military, AIDS/HIV education and intervention, Greg Louganis, and media representation opened up discussions during my visits and weekly phone calls. My male partner has been invited to important family gatherings, such as my parents' thirtieth-wedding-anniversary cruise to Mexico in 1996. He and I even shared a room with my parents when we took a vacation in Reno, Nevada. Through painful tears and constant dialogue, individual reflections and mutual understanding, my parents and I grew together and became closer. At last, I could fully share with my family and no longer had to live a separate life. I felt connected and at peace.

Coming out as bisexual and strongly identifying as queer introduced me to new allies, new responsibilities, and new directions in my activism. As an out queer coordinator of the Asian Pacific Student Programs office on campus, I was asked to be a member and then selected to be a co-chair of a chancellor's advisory committee that examined lesbian, gay, bisexual, and transgender issues and put forth policy and procedural recommendations to the administration. With the guidance of other committee members, I forwarded several points of action to our chancellor, which included processes of domestic partnership registration and benefits inclusion; support for the interdisciplinary minor in Gay, Lesbian, and Bisexual Studies; analysis of same-sex sexual harassment; and incorporation of transgenderism in the committee's name, scope, and activities. I had represented our campus in a statewide university steering committee and spearheaded a report that compiled information on campus contacts and community resources. I was also elected to be chair of the Bisexual Youth Initiative and a Pacific regional representative for BiNet USA, a national nonprofit group of bisexual advocates and organizations. In addition, I was selected to participate in the Youth Leadership Institute of the National Gay and Lesbian Task Force and addressed the 1997 Creating Change conference as a keynote speaker. In these settings, I gained new mentors, new communities, and renewed energy.

However, I could not help feeling that my racial and sexual identities were distinctly separated and purposely compartmentalized. I was the only out queer on the board of directors of a statewide Asian American and Pacific Islander organization composed of higher education administrators, faculty, staff, and students. I was noticeably one of the few Asian American and Pacific Islanders in the various queer organizations that I belonged to. In most cases, the agenda focused solely on race/ethnicity or on sexuality, depending on the organization, and often made no concrete correlation between the two. Although it easily can be argued that the history and experiences of people of color and queers have been different in significant ways, the system and operations of discrimination still remain intact and unchallenged. Our lack of coalition building and networking perpetuates the powerlessness of marginalized communities and plays into the dominant group's strategy of divide and conquer. And what about queers of color, like me? Where do I fit? Which parts of me belong and which ones are excluded? Am I fragmented, once again?

Even though I have been empowered to take action, frequently I feel alone. My bold attempts to raise topics of sexuality among people of color or issues of racism in queer groups have been met with quizzical looks, blatant denial, or patronizing dismissal. Similar to my experience in my predominantly white fraternity, my identity as a person of color is relegated to secondary priority in the predominantly white lesbian, gay, bisexual, and transgender organizations. The same is true in communities of color in which the topic of sexuality and nonheterosexual perspectives are hardly discussed. I search endlessly for ways to simultaneously address race and sexuality because as a Filipino bi-queer man these identities and issues converge at the same time for and within me. I am both Filipino and queer. I can no longer accept the rationale and excuses that explain why communities of color and queer communities cannot come together or join in alliances without shifting or diluting their individual agendas. I can no longer tolerate heterosexism in communities of color or white supremacy in queer communities. I do not believe we can label an individual, a group, or even a movement progressive if we do not take into consideration its impact on other social-justice groups or the cost of its success.

I look for a place that embraces, respects, and values my multiple and overlapping identities, experiences, and politics. I am an immigrant from the Philippines, a proud product of affirmative action and bilingual education programs, a bi-queer man involved in an interracial relationship, college-educated, from a working-class family, an educator and writer committed to social justice and raising critical consciousness. I do not prioritize my identities or claim to speak for the communities that I belong to. I am limited to my own experiences, readings, and interactions with others. Yet, I search continuously for better understanding, linkage, cooperation, and harmony. I join other sisters and brothers who challenge, provoke, and defy, comrades who no longer wait but work for change and justice, those I could count on as family members who are also looking for a place to call home.

5

You're a What? An Activist??

Alain Anh-Tuan Dang

Over the years, I have organized or participated in numerous campaigns for social justice. The mid- to late 1990s saw a resurgence of student activism in California. From attacks on affirmative action in the University of California system, to attacks on people of color through electoral politics, the struggles of the 1990s cultivated a new generation of activists. I use the term *activist* with its most inclusive definition in mind. I believe a person can be an activist in many forms. From organizing a mass rally against hate crimes, to sponsoring neighbors in annual walk-a-thons, such actions effect change, and therefore can be considered activism. As I reflect on my community "activism" of recent years I struggle with many questions. Foremost in my mind are the questions: Why am I an activist? What factors have led me to take this difficult journey in life? Let me tell you my story. Together, maybe we can make some sense of it.

I grew up in Cupertino, California, an affluent community in the heart of Silicon Valley. It is a community where nearly everyone is somehow connected to the technology industry. It is a community that families seek out because of the "excellent" public schools. Its civic-minded residents take part in numerous cultural celebrations annually. It is the classic idealized suburban town of "American dreams."

Cupertino is a socially homogeneous, if not an ethnically homogeneous community. In my years growing up, I never felt I was different than any other kid in my school. The schools I attended were nearly half white and half Asian/Pacific American. I thought every family was like mine. I thought every family ate dinner together around eight in the evening and that a staple of every meal was rice. Every weekend my family would eat *pho* (a type of Vietnamese noodle soup) in

San Jose. Again, I thought every family did the same. Nearly all the Asian families in Cupertino were of Chinese descent. As I grew up during prosperous economic times, racial tensions were minimal.

My picture-perfect adolescence was spent on the soccer field, playing AYSO (American Youth Soccer Organization) soccer after school. Weekly soccer practices, intermingled with piano and voice lessons, made for busy afternoons. With high school came a stronger focus on music. I went to Monta Vista High School. At the time, it was known for its music department. I enjoyed four years of performing on stage in plays and musicals and, in my senior year, singing with the locally renowned Madrigals. My passion for performing was so strong that I considered majoring in music in college. Although this dream of mine to perform persists to this day, I realized I had to make some "practical" choices in my life, hence the idea of majoring in music had to go. Picturing me as such a happy and active youth, one would probably not immediately point and say, "There is a future activist!"

Fast-forward to college. In the fall of 1994, I entered the University of California, Irvine (UCI), with a major in social ecology. That fall, voters in California passed Proposition 187, the so-called "Save our State" initiative. That proposition, which has since been thrown out by the courts, declared undocumented immigrants ineligible for numerous public services. It was the first in a long string of electoral attacks on people of color and other minorities that included Propositions 209, the antiaffirmative action initiative; 227, the antibilingual education initiative; 21, the so-called "juvenile justice" initiative; and 22, the antigay marriage initiative. At that time, I was still politically unconscious. All I cared about was fitting in and making friends with the many people around me who came from varied backgrounds. Although we lived in the epitome of suburbia—Irvine, California—there was much diversity in the life experiences among the friends I made. I saw college as a prime opportunity to start anew. But anew from what? What didn't I like about my life in Cupertino?

One could say my activism began in the Greek system at UCI. In the winter of 1996 I was seeking an opportunity to get more involved in school. A call went out to start a chapter of a national Greek fraternity at my campus. I answered that call and before I knew it, I was the founding vice president of programming. I saw this as an opportunity to reform the Greek system. Hoping to move away from tradition,

I tried to bring a progressive perspective to the events I organized. One idea I pushed was a series of workshops on multiculturalism through service learning. I did not want the sole purpose of this chapter to be to enable its members to hook up with the opposite sex under the guise of philanthropy and networking. Unfortunately, this idea did not get off the ground because of opposition from fellow board members. They felt the UCI Greek system's single evening seminar on diversity was sufficient. Increasingly alienated from my "brothers" because of ideological differences, I left the chapter after one year. Trying to change an entrenched system was too large a task.

During this time I struggled not only with my brothers; I also struggled with myself in coming to grips with my sexuality. This was the beginning of a long process of personal identity formation, but it would soon be put on the back burner for some time.

In the summer of 1995, the University of California Board of Regents passed Standing Policies 1 and 2 (SP-1 and SP-2) banning affirmative action in admissions and hiring. Those actions touched off a firestorm of protests among students, faculty, staff, and communities statewide. I parlayed my participation in those protests into action in the fall of 1996, when I organized, in conjunction with the University of California Student Association, the student component of the "No on 209" campaign in Orange County. A bastion of political conservatism, Orange County proved a difficult place to defend affirmative action. I built a coalition among colleges in the area and spent much of my time going door to door, talking to folks about why I believed Prop 209 should be defeated. Although Proposition 209 passed statewide, it was defeated in every precinct in which I organized.

Like many other activists of that time, I took the defeat hard. We sacrificed blood, sweat, and tears to defeat 209. It was a physically and emotionally draining experience. However, I did not let this one defeat crush my spirit. I wanted to reexperience the inner passion and exhilaration I felt working on that campaign. That feeling returned one evening when I viewed a segment on Nike sweatshops in Vietnam on the TV show *48 Hours*. Women as young as fourteen years old worked under atrocious conditions and were paid pittance for sewing shoes. Meanwhile, Nike was ironically in the midst of its marketing campaign to champion female athletes. Watching the pain and feeling of helplessness among my sisters in Vietnam moved me to act once again. I could not just stand by and let this situation persist. I had to act.

I decided a multipronged campaign was in order. That year I sat on the Legislative Council for the Associated Students of UC Irvine. I cosponsored legislation that condemned Nike's practices overseas and effectively made UCI the first university to boycott Nike over its labor practices. At the same time, numerous forums and street-theater actions educated the campus community about the conditions under which university-licensed apparel was manufactured. The Vietnamese American Coalition, of which I was a member, spearheaded the movement. By the end of the campaign, more than 1,000 letters of protest were sent by UCI students to Nike CEO Phil Knight, and the university chose not to renew contracts with Nike. Since the UCI campaign, universities across the country have organized against the use of sweatshop labor in university-licensed apparel. The University of California is the largest university so far to adopt a code of conduct for the manufacture of its licensed apparel.

I took these organizing experiences and integrated them into my work ethic. After four years in southern California I decided to move back to the Bay Area. I quickly immersed myself in community work and accumulated an eclectic resume of experiences organizing against sweatshops, facilitating intercultural communication, working as a staff assistant in a congressional district office, joining a queer youth speakers bureau, and more. These endeavors continue to shape my identity, whether professional or personal.

Why am I giving you my abridged life story? At first glance it would seem unlikely that a boy growing up in Cupertino would engage in activism. What was his motivation? Why would he struggle to fight for fairness and equality? In answer to these questions, perhaps his own personal struggle in accepting his queer identity was the impetus for his activism. That is the conclusion I have come to in assessing my life. I fight against oppression as a means to fight my own oppression.

How was I oppressed? High school is a difficult time for youth. But for queer youth buried deep in the closet it can be an especially tumultuous experience. I knew I was gay, but I had no one I could confide in, let alone explore these feelings with. I lived life in complete denial of who I was. As a queer youth, lying became second nature to me. I lied about myself to everyone. I went through the motions of what was "accepted": I participated in student life, activities. I even went to the prom. But the entire time I felt I was undercover, living life as I felt I should, not as how I wanted to live. I built walls around me and did not let many people in. It's sad to say that I left Cupertino with numerous acquaintances but few people I regarded as true friends. The neighborhood I lived in was not hospitable to queer youth. This was a community of hyper-heterosexuality, "family values," and social conformity. My greatest performance as an actor was my high school experience.

Although activism is often seen as altruistic, for me it felt more personal. The activism I began in college was a reaction to my stifling experience growing up in suburbia. By engaging in activism, working to end injustice in the world around me, perhaps I felt I could overcome the obstacles I faced in forming a positive self-identity. I needed to see for myself that individuals could change society and that this change to a better society would include acceptance of people like me. This process of self-acceptance took more than four years to bring me to a point where I was comfortable enough with myself to finally live my life openly as a queer Asian/Pacific American man.

The contradictions of living as a queer man in the United States and as an Asian/Pacific American in the United States still haunt me. I hate playing the "how oppressed are you" game, but there is some truth to differentiating personal oppressions. It is not easy living as a minority within a minority. Queer communities can be as racist as Asian/Pacific American communities can be heterosexist. I am always questioning where I fit in this matrix. Through activism and by letting myself be labeled as an activist, I am sent to the fringes of both communities. Although activists have a role in society to agitate "the masses" into action, they are not seen yet as mainstream forces for change. Could I be more effective in my work by not allowing myself to be labeled an activist? Would my opinions not be so easily discounted as those of someone who is expected to question authority?

Engaging in activism in Asian/Pacific American communities often pits my loyalty to them against my loyalty to queer communities. Even among activists, I feel torn between conflicting worldviews. For instance, some Asian/Pacific American activists I have worked with hold strong beliefs about traditional family roles. I have found myself in numerous situations in which I have felt silenced or left out because the focus of conversation was on working to better the community for our children. I, too, want to better communities for our children, but some activists cling to the patriarchal notion that the future generations we are fighting for grow up in nuclear families, a notion that is far from the reality today of families existing in various forms. In this respect, I sometimes am challenged working in Asian/Pacific American communities.

Socializing among members of young, queer Asian/Pacific American communities has presented its own challenges. Coming out is like a second adolescence—as if it wasn't hard enough the first time around. Building relationships, friendships, trust, and intimacy must be relearned in queer contexts. For example, many queer men I associate with are fashion-conscious. For them, it is important to present the image of success, and for many this means showing that they are trendsetters: Brand-name identification sets these queer men apart from the crowd. My work against sweatshops placed me a number of times in situations where I have felt intense peer pressure. I have been questioned as to why I am against fashion. I am not against fashion, I am against the exploitative nature of apparel manufacturing. In this instance, my activism puts me at odds with members of my communities. A lot of my friends are themselves activists. They work with queer youth, helping develop positive self-images among those just coming out of the closet. As activists, how do we recognize and integrate work on different issues when they may appear to be in conflict with one another? How do I reconcile my work on the sweatshop front with my work in queer communities? This is just one example in which the visibility of my work exposes conflicts within my communities. My friends use fashion as a means to assert their queer identity. However, their consumptive habits that enable this identity conflict with the goals and objectives of my activism.

Tunnel vision is a problem in many activist circles I have encountered. Groups and organizations are so focused on their particular issue that it becomes difficult for them to see themselves as part of a larger progressive movement. Most organizations are singular in focus, whether that focus be on politics, social services, health care, counseling, support, what have you. They spend all their efforts advocating for themselves (which often centers on narrow notions of who they are) and sometimes do not realize that by doing so another group or a subgroup may lose out. Competition for resources, particularly money, is often seen as a zero-sum situation. If one group gains, then conversely another must lose.

These conflicting paradigms typify my life. Whether I am speaking to student groups about tolerance—no, *acceptance*—of my queer brothers and sisters, or lobbying on behalf of a number of issues, I am constantly checking myself and trying to stay true to my values. We each live life balancing on a high wire, trying to maintain an inner equilibrium between our intellectual and emotional selves. Often I feel as if I am being pulled in opposite directions. Having engaged in activism in both Asian/Pacific American and queer communities, I have come to see these communities as working toward similar goals, albeit taking differing paths. In the end, we are all seeking social, economic, and political justice.

The experiences I describe here have just begun to shape my existence. I take pieces of everything that has happened and carry them with me. I have not forgotten the people I have interacted with on one level or another. Every conversation, even the fleeting ones, is not insignificant. I am not so conceited as to think that I got to where I am in life by myself. I believe building relationships is the foundation of social change. If I am to continue to fight and struggle for change, I must always build on my past to construct a solid foundation for the future.

The story of my life is a work in progress. I cannot imagine a life for myself marked by apathy or complacency. It is my core belief that I, as an individual working in concert with others, will make some concrete changes in this world. I envision a society in which individuality is celebrated, in which each unique person is appreciated as an integral part of the collective whole. I hope one day to realize this dream. I hope that all people will be valued regardless of race, gender, sexual orientation, culture, ability, or any other societal marker. I know this is asking for much, but I can still dream, can't I?

6

On Becoming a Bi Bi Grrrl

Wei Ming Dariotis

I have three stories to tell. They explain how I came to know myself as bisexual and as Asian American, or rather, as hapa (literally meaning "part" in Hawaiian, hapa was originally used in hapa haole to indicate someone of mixed Native Hawaiian and European heritage, and now has come to mean an Asian American and/or Pacific Islander of mixed heritage, as in EuroAsian, AfroAsian, Latin-Asian, Native-Asian, or any API mix). The stories explain how I came to identify as a bi hapa (as in, "don't worry, bi hapa"), and how I came to know myself as a bi bi grrrl. They are true, but no single story is the whole truth. They need one another to make sense, intellectually and emotionally, just as I need both my attraction to men and women and my attraction to other Asian Americans to make sense of who I am in the world.

Story #1

It was my first year of college (at Wesleyan University in Connecticut, where I spent that first year, it is never called fresh*man* year). I was away from my home in San Francisco for the first time, and, oddly enough, it was when I was away from this queer capital of America, this capital of Asian America, and this hapa heaven that I finally realized these identities to be my own.

Let me clarify: not only am I bisexual, but I am also hapa. My mother is Chinese and my biological father is Greek Swedish Scottish English German. Although I knew this when I was growing up— I mean, just look at my name (first name, Chinese, last name, Greek)—I still didn't really think of myself as Chinese, and certainly not as hapa, a word I didn't even know then.

Sure, I lived in predominantly Chinese San Francisco on the edge of Chinatown. My mom is first-generation Chinese from Hong Kong. My stepfather is a fourth-generation Chinese American, the son of a "paper son" (which means his father bought papers that said he belonged to someone else's family tree in order to circumvent the Chinese Exclusion Act). I even have a Chinese American little brother. But all this did was show me how Chinese or even Chinese American I was not. I didn't look like I fit into the picture. People would see our little family and think my mom, my stepfather, and my brother fit each other.

But who was I?

One of these things is not like the others. One of these things is not the same.

I was raised vegetarian because my (white) father followed a Sikh Master; it was part of his 1960s thing, just like avoiding the draft for Vietnam (which is why I was born in Australia) and marrying his Chinese girlfriend (which is why I was born). So I couldn't eat anything at my stepfather's Chinese family banquets. Through thirteen courses I would sit there asking for, "Another bowl of rice, please?" I may have been the only Chinese person there using a Chinese first name, but it was clear to everyone that, whatever I was, I was not Chinese.

So when I got to Wesleyan I already knew what I wasn't, but I just didn't know what I was.

I still don't know how it happened, but someone convinced me to go to a meeting of the Asian American student group on campus. Wesleyan had only one group for Asian Americans, unlike San Francisco State University, where I now teach, which has more than thirty; seven just for Filipino students. I went, and instead of being surrounded by Chinese Americans who spoke Cantonese and whose grandparents had been held on Angel Island, I was surrounded by East Coast Asian Americans who all knew the same basics I did—how to use chopsticks, and also how, when someone asks you what you are, you say, "American." Suddenly I didn't have anything to prove.

I started to understand that I didn't have to be exactly like the Chinese Americans in Chinatown who I saw as "authentic," my vision having been influenced by the media. I also didn't have to try, however subtly, to pass as only white. Like many of the East Coast Asian

Americans I met, I had grown up thinking I was white-ish (or maybe Jewish). I did not consciously wish to pass for "white," which was something I knew I could never really be. But I did imagine myself to be a kind of European "ethnic"—Greek, Italian, Spanish, Jewish, the kind of people I was frequently mistaken to be. It wasn't that I wanted to be any of those things so much as I just felt that I wasn't Chinese.

I had been so caught up in feeling not-Chinese that I couldn't comprehend the possibility of being Chinese-and-something. So things really changed for me in college. I started to understand that I could be "Asian American." And as I began to understand intellectually that I was Asian American, I also began to understand my multiracial position in the world. (I use "racial" to mean one of the five major constructed categories that divide and limit the lives of people, although I believe in only one human "race.")

To begin to see myself as Chinese American in a positive sense, I had to accept that my European heritage was part of who I am; who I am is both of these things, double, not just half. Slowly it dawned on me that my parents had transgressed some kind of racial boundary reminiscent of antimiscegenation laws, which prohibited marriage between European Americans and other groups in order to maintain a sense of the purity of whiteness. In creating me, they were tainting the white race. That boundary—between "white" and other—is the only structural racial boundary in this country because even though there is prejudice between groups of people of color, the divisions meant to maintain "white purity" are the only ones to have been institutionalized and legalized.

This realization made me wonder, "If I am the product of two people who said it doesn't matter who you love, then why stop at race? What about gender?" Wesleyan was the perfect place for such ruminations.

In my first week of college, I was led through a sensitivity training exercise. In this exercise, the participants sat in a circle and told their "coming out" stories, using their real lives as material. For some people this exercise was play-acting, but for others it was a safe space to tell their stories. As a group of eighteen-year-olds trying to impress one another with how cool we were, we did okay. But I still remember how terrifying it was to say, "My name is Wei Ming, and I am a lesbian." We didn't have the choice of saying bisexual. The woman who led us through the exercise, CS (you'll see later why I remember her name fourteen years after the fact), was herself bisexual, but she told us that for the exercise to really work, heterosexuals in the group had to move completely outside of our comfort zones and gays and lesbians had to be given a really safe space. At the time I accepted this, but now I see it as a negation of the experience of bisexuals. On the other hand, when my students do this exercise I know many of them choose the bisexual option because it does make the exercise more comfortable for them.

As a bisexual hapa, I see parallels between this exercise and my question about Asian American identity: Does a hapa "count" as a full Asian American? We have benefits our "full" sisters and brothers (in my case, literally, as my brother is not hapa) don't have. Some Eurasians have a certain amount of white privilege because they "look white" (which, of course, often depends on who is doing the looking). Some of us who are visibly "of color" can still have white privilege indirectly through our families and our heritage. In this country there are different varieties of racism, depending on whether a person looks Latino, African American, Native American, or Asian American. Since hapas often look anything but Asian American, we may find ourselves experiencing racism or privilege differently than "full" APIs.

As hapas, we are not white, just as bisexuals are not heterosexual. To be told that we "can pass" is worse than an insult; it just doesn't make sense. What would it mean for me to "pass" for white or heterosexual? What part of myself would I be "passing by"? Sure, many hapas could "pass" if they tried hard enough, and perhaps some do simply by not asserting their Asian/Pacific American (APA) heritage. But I won't try to "pass" because I know who and what I am. To "pass" would be to lose myself.

I'll admit it—I didn't make all of these connections just from the exercise CS led me through, but that is definitely the moment it all started to come together. Before it hit me on an intellectual level it got to me emotionally, or maybe just in my gut. That exercise gave me the tools to continue to work these issues out. I may not, to this day, feel "fully" Chinese American, but I most certainly am Asian American, partially by virtue of being hapa. I participate fully in my Asian American communities as a member of several APA community arts organizations and through Hapa Issues Forum, a nonprofit activist and support organization dedicated to creating meaningful dialogue on issues concerning Asians of mixed heritage and challenging this nation's rigid notions of race (for more info, check out the Web site at www.hapaissuesforum.org). In addition to being bisexual, CS is hapa Eurasian. She is doubly like me. I never got to know her very well but something about the way these racial and sexual identities were merged in her struck a chord in me. Just last month, I received an e-mail from her because she was interested in submitting to the anthology that I'm co-editing, *Bi Bi Grrrls: Bisexual/Biracial Women Speak Out.*

But this is just Story #1, the prelude that allows Story #2 to happen.

Story #2

It was my first year in college. It was my first time on the East Coast. My roommate was from Maine. We had been matched up pretty well by our resident advisor (RA) (we had the same peach and cream comforter, the same set of blue and white dishes, and we were the only ones on our floor to bring an ironing board and iron), but we were also very different. Her ancestors had come over on the Mayflower. My mom came over on a Boeing. Looking through her high school yearbook, I remarked, "There don't seem to be very many nonwhite people at your school." Her response: "There was this Jewish girl once." Huh? My high school in San Francisco allowed optional attendance on important Jewish holidays. I had learned to sing the dreidel song at the same time I learned to say Gung Hay Fat Choy (Happy New Year) in second grade. So we did have some fundamental differences. But basically we got along very well. And then there was this month-long winter break. I was with my parents, and I suppose I should have been thinking about my boyfriend, but instead all I could think about was my roommate and the thirty-minute hug we had before we left for break. One of our hallmates had shouted, "Why don't you two get a room?" and we both just smiled and kept on hugging.

So when we got back to school for spring semester, I put all of that intellectualizing into action and embarked on an affair with my roommate. How did it happen? Wouldn't you like to know! Let's say it started off being "very bisexual"—in other words, there was a guy in the room with us. I feel sorry for him, in retrospect, because neither of us was as interested in him as we were in each other. She and I made love regularly for the rest of the school year. We caused quite a scandal, revealing that, despite the care with which roommates are matched up, the heterosexist assumptions of the administrators did not allow for the possibility that they were in fact matchmaking.

Was I a lesbian? No. In the same way that I knew I was not Chinese, I knew I wasn't exclusively a lover of women (although I do identify as a woman-loving woman). I had been, as one friend from high school put it, too "rampantly heterosexual" for that. So, I am bisexual. Queer. Hapa. APA.

To be bisexual is to be queer. To be hapa is to be Asian/Pacific American.

What did I do with all these identities?

I transferred back to the West Coast—the East Coast winters killed me (was it ever anything but winter?). In my junior year at the University of Washington, I thought I finally had a chance to put all of my self-knowledge into political practice. I signed up to be a resident advisor in the dorms. I could run all of the sensitivity exercises and community-building games that my RA at Wesleyan had done.

I got a floor with fifty students, mostly sophomores, mostly male, mostly white (except for the two hapas trying to pass for white—yes, blue contact lenses and everything). Many were in the ROTC. After the first floor meeting I quickly put away the idea of doing the "coming-out" exercise. I'm glad that I did: After they found out I was a vegetarian from San Francisco, some residents taped a granola bar to my door. It was not meant to be a gift.

This was just the opening salvo in what turned out to be a constant, low-level war.

I had come out to my mother almost as soon as I decided I was bisexual. But I could not come out to my residents. In fact, quite the opposite, I made sure my boyfriend was a visible presence in the hall because I became very, very afraid. The head resident advisor of my dorm was an out lesbian, and she decided to start a support group for queer students living in the dorm. The group was called "One in Ten" and all of the RAs in the dorm started putting up flyers to advertise the group's meetings. The ones on my floor were torn down (and violently shredded into confetti) within two hours of being put up. In their place, someone pasted a *Playboy* centerfold on the hallway mirror, and beneath it a sign reading, "Nine out of ten of us like to fuck somebody of the opposite sex."

My boyfriend started hanging around a lot more.

I used him as a security blanket. I wonder if I would have even stayed with him for the whole year if I hadn't needed what I thought of as his protection from the homophobia that surrounded me. What if I had had a girlfriend at the time? Or had not been with anyone? What privilege of safety did my bisexuality—and my apparent heterosexuality—afford me? In the same way, I downplayed being Asian. I mean, I didn't change my name, but I didn't bring up those issues either. I didn't challenge every racist and sexist remark, although I did try to do so about half of the time, maybe more. But I felt like I was in a war zone, and I didn't feel like I had the luxury of being brave. Yes, I "can pass." But at what cost? A year later when I was living in Seattle's gay neighborhood, Samoan gangs were reputedly going around gay bashing. Queer groups were out walking defensive perimeters. I walked home in the dark tense every night, prepared to show whatever identity, queer or Asian, straight or bi, would get me home safely.

A year after my tour of duty in the dorms I saw the head homophobe from my floor standing with a group of lesbians I knew from a women's studies course on lesbianism I had taken. This guy, this homophobia instigator, smiled when he saw me. Me. He walked toward me and said, "Wei Ming, I have to apologize to you for all the stuff I did last year. I was just realizing I was bisexual and I wasn't handling it very well. I didn't want anyone to know, so I was acting as tough as I could be."

I tell this story now to my classes before we do the "coming-out" exercise. It's a kind of warning: "If you act too homophobic, everyone will think you are gay." So I use homophobia to prevent its outward expression, because the hardest thing is to get them to really do the exercise. Once they just do it, things can start to sink in. Things can start to open up. *They* can start to open up.

I do this exercise in the context of Asian American studies classes because that is what I teach now. No matter what the subject of the course—Asians of Mixed Heritage, Asian American Women, Asian American Composition—I fit it in because it does fit. Queer issues are part of Asian/Pacific American life the way Asian Americans are part of "American" life. We're here. Get used to it.

I used to think to be an activist I had to be on the streets with banners and signs and shout myself hoarse. Sometimes I still do that kind of activism, but sometimes it is the presence of my body, queer and hapa, that is making the statement. Activism is contextual, and it is something everyone can do in different ways in different situations.

You may not always have to come out, although my coming out as bi in my position as professor has, I think, changed people's lives. Once, after I did it fearfully, a student I had not known was gay came up to me and thanked me because it made him feel safe in a way he never had before in a classroom. After that, I made it a standing policy to get it out there as much as possible. I decided to make my students comfortable with the idea of my bisexuality, and the need not to be heterosexist, or homophobic (or, for that matter, biphobic) in my classroom, and hopefully beyond.

Many of my students come to me already actualized as antiracist activists, but they may not see how being antiracist must be connected to being antimisogynist and antihomophobic. In fact, too often I have heard cultural-nationalist rhetoric that is very antiracist but that is also both misogynist and homophobic. In college, a fellow APA activist told me and a large group of our peers, "The man and the woman are the basic unit of the community, and if you break up that unit, you break up the community." In other words, "You can't talk about Yellow Pride and sleep white." Queer people, in this schema, destroy the community because they break up the stability of the man-woman unit. It should come as no surprise that this stability is based on the superiority of the man in the dyad. My students sometimes ask,

> Can we really fight all of those things at the same time? Don't we need to concentrate our efforts on the thing we see most clearly—racism? Can't the gays and women just wait until we gain equality in terms of race first? We don't need the distraction, the division of our energies.

To that, I have some of my own questions: Does being queer make you any less Asian American? Does being a woman make you any less Asian American? Where do we draw the lines of authenticity? Of inclusion and exclusion? And when we draw those lines, aren't we diluting our power? Who we are as people, Asian/Pacific American, is diverse by definition. We have to embrace it, because therein lies our strength. We cannot ignore the issues brought to our attention by women, by queers, by South Asians, by hapas or anyone else, and define them as issues that do not immediately belong in our APA community. We have to embrace those issues because they are our issues. Is the history of the internment camp relevant only to Japanese Americans? Does the history of Chinese exclusion affect only Chinese Americans? What happens now happens to all of us. What we can make happen is an understanding that we will not be divided along these or any other lines. Make the circle bigger. And bigger.

I make queer issues part of the dialogue in my work within Asian-American communities through such groups as Hapa Issues Forum and Kearny Street Workshop, which is the oldest multidisciplinary panethnic APA arts organization and is rooted in the community struggle to save the International Hotel. I do similar things when hanging out and talking about relationships—I remind my friends (gently) that I am not interested only in men. Or in women.

To what degree is language just language?

When does speech become action?

When it changes people's minds.

I am bisexual. I am hapa. I am the product of two people deciding that racial boundaries should not get in their way. I have decided that race isn't the only boundary I need to cross personally or politically.

Story #3

My mother (this wouldn't be a Chinese American woman's story without her mother, would it?) used to be racist and homophobic. When I was ten she would tell me not to bring my black friend home. She would tell me, "Don't get tan; you'll look like a Mexican." She would say awful things about our gay neighbors, even when I would argue with her because my best friend at the time was a girl who had been adopted by nice lesbian people.

People change.

My mom and I have always had a very good, non–*Joy Luck Club* kind of relationship. Despite her prejudices, I knew I could still tell her things, so I did. I told her when I first fell in love with a woman. I told her my opinion about her racism. She listened.

When my much younger brother was about ten years old, he came home one day calling a classmate of his a "fag." My mother called me two days later to tell me:

> You would be very proud of me. I told Alex he can't talk like
> that. I told him he might be very popular right now, but tomor-
> row it could turn around and then, because he is Chinese, they
> could call him a Chink, and it is just like calling the other kid a
> fag.

I was very proud of her, not only for correcting my brother, but also
for making a connection between racism and homophobia—they are
oppressions that support each other. This is why we need to work on
eliminating both of them, at the same time. She's had a few more opportunities to impress me as well. Later that same year a teacher at
my brother's school tried to teach human sexuality as a continuum,
including bisexuality and homosexuality. Several parents became
very upset and tried to convince other parents to pressure the school's
principal to fire the teacher. My mother found out about the contro-
versy one day when, while picking up my brother, she was approached by another mother who asked her to get involved in getting
the teacher fired. My mom turned to this woman and told her,

> Think about the mistake you are making. You are only harming
> yourself because your daughter may turn out to be a lesbian, and
> if she sees how much prejudice you have, she might hate herself
> enough to take her own life. Or she might just stop talking to
> you. Either way, you would lose your daughter. And even if you
> think this wouldn't happen to you, why waste so much energy
> being so hateful toward others?

Activism can go further than you think. The ripples can go in many
directions, even in the directions you aren't looking.

Now I understand that becoming a bi bi grrrl, a bisexual hapa feminist, is a process of enacting my identities. It isn't just about me and
how I see myself or how I ask others to see me. It's also about being a
part of communities. I wouldn't exist without my communities to
support me, so I need to support them. My communities include my
family. My communities include people I may not at first see as being
like me. My job is to recognize our connections and to create them,
and to encourage the same from others.

How is my story like and unlike yours? Where do our identities
and communities intersect? What can you do to make these connections stronger? What will you do now?

7

My Multiple Identity Disorder

TC Duong

A lot has been said about how the United States is quickly moving to be "majority minority," where the total number of people of color will outnumber whites in this country. But what does "minority" mean in a country where the numbers of people of color are growing every day? California is already "majority minority" because of immigration across the Mexican border and from Asian countries.

I grew up in Orange County, California, home to the largest number of Vietnamese in the United States. My family came to the United States in 1975 with the first wave of Vietnamese immigration, moving around the country until 1980 when we settled down in Irvine, California. Irvine was an example of the "typical" southern California suburb: racially diverse, economically homogenous. I grew up with a lot of access to "my culture." Little Saigon in nearby Westminster was the center of an extensive and growing Vietnamese American community. Like Chinatowns in other cities, Little Saigon had Vietnamese hairdressers, grocery stores, restaurants, bookstores, cafes, and pharmacies.

Discussions about race in Orange County, with its large Southeast Asian and Latino populations, differ from discussions about race in the mainstream United States. Dialogue in mainstream society often centers on black and white, and ignores dynamics between Asian Americans/Pacific Islanders (AAPIs) and whites, as well as AAPI-Latino, AAPI-Native American, and AAPI-black dynamics. I remember going to a conference where a speaker talking about the media and GLBTQ people of color said that the way television deals with people of color is to "ghetto-ize" them by giving them their own show. Now correct me if I'm wrong, but a sitcom about the wacky Native American family has not aired. And other than the canceled

"All-American Girl," television shows centered on AAPIs are also nonexistent.

In the affluent suburb that is Irvine, I grew up surrounded by different races and ethnicities but talked rarely about racial dynamics. As a good liberal, I tried (in vain) to get Dukakis elected, wrote letters to ban the use of gill nets, and lobbied for youth representation on the city council. Never did I actually think about the issues that the Vietnamese American community faced. Looking back, I see now that I viewed activism as a white person's activity and so I left my identity as a Vietnamese American behind.

When I came out as bisexual, I rarely spent time with other AAPIs, much less other Vietnamese Americans. Doing activism in white queer communities meant I could maintain the long-established disconnect between activism and my Vietnamese American identity. While I connected with GLBTQ activists who were fighting against silence and oppression, it became clear that my identity as a person of color was rarely if ever taken into account as one of the barriers I faced. Because I am a U.S. citizen, spent much time living in the United States, and am upper-middle class, I had the "luxury" of "passing" and putting my Vietnamese heritage in the background. In fact, someone I volunteered with actually told me that they had forgotten I was a person of color. In my years of working and volunteering for GLBTQ organizations, I have had to make a conscious effort to bring my identity and issues of racism forward. The major barrier for queer AAPIs is a double-minority status that doubles our invisibility. For GLBTQ AAPIs, we are invisible within both the larger GLBTQ communities and the AAPI communities. For families dealing with a loved one's sexual orientation or gender identity, culturally appropriate resources in either community are scarce. My parents certainly didn't have any institutions or resources in the Vietnamese American community that could help them deal with my sexuality.

I met Harold and Ellen Kameya through my work as a field manager for Parents, Families, and Friends of Lesbians and Gays (PFLAG). As with my parents, the Kameyas told me that when their daughter Valerie came out as a lesbian, their first feeling was one of isolation. None of the organizations in the Japanese American community in southern California addressed issues of sexual orientation. As Harold says, "This issue had not been discussed in the Japanese American press, nor in our Japanese American church. We knew, however, that it was not a topic that was safe to discuss." In my organizing work I also face this lack of resources and information about sexuality in AAPI communities. During a community meeting for AAPI organizations in Washington, DC, I asked a pastor of a predominantly Chinese church about what kind of support they offered regarding sexual orientation and gender identity issues. The answer was, predictably, "none."

Unfortunately, support and resources are also scarce within predominantly white GLBTQ organizations. As happens in so many predominantly white spaces, people of color (along with other oppressed people) often have to leave their "other" identities at the door when predominantly white organizations are not prepared to address their unique (cultural) needs. The Kameyas initially went to the Los Angeles chapter of PFLAG to get support for dealing with their daughter's coming out. While they found the anonymity of being in an all-white space comforting, Harold and Ellen again felt isolated, being the only people of color in the room. There were no culturally sensitive resources in AAPI languages that were available for families to take back into their homes. When Harold and Ellen decided to reach out to other Asian families, they dealt with a lack of comfort with bringing up personal issues with strangers. For AAPI families, the PFLAG model of support groups is one that is not always culturally appropriate. The racist assumptions from GLBTQ communities that communities of color are more homophobic and transphobic than white communities were also barriers for the families that Harold and Ellen wanted to support. Other baggage that people of color deal with when in predominantly white spaces, such as issues of tokenism, being asked to speak for your whole race, and being called a "credit" to your community were all barriers that the Kameyas and other people of color within PFLAG faced.

In response, the Kameyas tried to create their own support groups specifically for GLBTQ AAPIs and their families. Over the years they struggled alone to develop an ongoing community for families of queer AAPIs. Their experience was that people would get one-on-one support or go to one meeting and never come back. That has changed recently with their partnership with Gay Asian Pacific Support Network (GAPSN). In the past few months they have had twenty to thirty people come to their support meetings. The partnership has

raised visibility for both the Kameyas' work and GAPSN and helps
provide support for many AAPI families in Los Angeles.

PFLAG As an Ally

Part of my work at PFLAG has been to help chapters learn how to
be allies of GLBTQ people of color and recognize their dual identities. In the process of reaching out to families of color, PFLAG realized that simply trying to include people of color in PFLAG may not
work. The work of challenging heterosexism and transphobia in communities of color has to happen on at least two levels. First, predominantly white organizations need to look at internal barriers and examine how their power structure, language, and resources are preventing
oppressed people from participating. PFLAG is working to examine
issues of racism within the organization and open the dialogue on
how white people can ally with the work of people of color. Issues
such as where the chapter meets, how the chapter provides support,
and how people of color are tokenized are being addressed. Also,
PFLAG has recently put together "Nuestras Hijas Y Nuestros Hijos,"
a Spanish-language adaptation of its resource pamphlet, "Our Daughters, Our Sons," as a first step in being culturally competent for Latino
communities.

The other way that challenging heterosexism and transphobia in
communities of color can happen is through the actual work of people of color. Across the country, I see GLBTQ people of color and
their family members creating culturally specific ways to support Latino, African-American, Native American, Arab, and AAPI families.
Each of these projects is designed for their specific communities.
For example, in Washington, DC, which is predominantly African
American, activists formed a support group specifically for African-American families. In Seattle, where there is no dominant community of color, activists have done outreach to the various Latino,
AAPI, and African-American communities.

Cross-Cultural Communication

Most of the time, racism and people of color are discussed in relation to white communities. However, in January 2001, I was part of a
group of people of color that came together to discuss the formation
of the Families of Color Network. This was one of the first times that

GLBTQ people of color and their allies have come together to share their experiences and strategize about working as a coalition for families. The discussion of how we as people of color can work together was a difficult and inspiring one. When we added issues of adultism and transphobia, our discussions became even deeper and more complex.

Throughout our time together, we talked about what each group needs from allies and how each could be an ally of other groups. We learned about each other's deep-seated anxieties and fears of racism across our communities. Many Native Americans did not want to be labeled as the bearers of spirituality. Many mixed-race people did not want to be asked to choose their racial category. Many Latinos in the room said that being labeled as "sex machines" was a barrier for someone asking to be an ally. Many AAPI people feared ethnicity would not be recognized, often hearing from potential allies phrases such as, "You don't act Asian." Many people across groups said they never wanted to hear that they "spoke so well," or be seen as homogenous, ignoring the various cultures within a particular racial or ethnic category. And finally, no one wanted to have an ally lump all people of color together and ignore the differences between cultures. It was a powerful beginning to the creation of a network that could be a national voice for families of GLBTQ people of color and provide support and resources to all of our racial and ethnic groups. We're still working on it, but just having the dialogue was a mind-blowing start.

It's a tricky thing to want to be seen as an individual and not be tokenized, and also want to be recognized as a person of color. I always cringe when I hear what I term as a "Connie Chung-ism," when a person of color (most likely an AAPI person) says he or she doesn't want to be known as an Asian American reporter/ writer/singer/actor/ activist. Most of the time this person has enough economic and class privilege that they believe race is less and less a factor. To me, there's internalized racism in such statements, as if being known as Asian American were somehow diminishing. But on the other hand, do I want to be known as a representative of my race? Can I as a bisexual, feminist, Vietnamese American, with full citizenship, no discernible accent, affluent parents, and a college education, speak for a recently immigrated, Laotian, transgender, female-to-male (FTM) youth?

What is so powerful about being in any queer people of color space is that I don't have to choose which part of my identity to leave behind. My identities are all a part of me even though I am often asked to leave some or all of them behind. By creating such spaces and developing allies, I hope that AAPI people and people of color will never have to leave their identities behind.

8

South of Normal

Loren R. Javier

I was born in Decatur, Illinois. Most people don't know where that is, but I like to say I was born south of Normal (Illinois, that is . . .). I've always meant it in a tongue-in-cheek way, just to be campy, but when I think about it, being born "south of normal" meant many things to me during the course of my lifetime.

When I was growing up, being "south of normal" meant I was "different." I was desperately trying to find the roads that intersected with everybody else. I never quite felt like I fit the conventional sense of "normal."

Oh, I got up every morning, went to school, played with my friends, went to soccer practice, watched cartoons on Saturday morning, and saw *Star Wars* more times than you can imagine. On the surface, I was living the "American dream." But, at the same time, I felt very different from the kids around me. I was a Filipino American kid growing up in the Midwest and, little by little, I was becoming more and more aware of my attraction to other boys.

The media played a large part in my life when I was younger (and it still does). I mean, what child wasn't weaned on television, the electric babysitter? I was riveted by shows such as *The Six Million Dollar Man, Fantasy Island,* and *Charlie's Angels.* Basically, white heroes and white people falling in love.

I was even lucky enough to get to watch shows that were deemed too risqué for my friends to watch. For example, the soap opera spoof *Soap* was a perennial favorite in the Javier household.

While we all laughed at the antics of the Campbells and the Tates (*Soap*'s central families), I couldn't help but be intrigued by the character of Jodie, played by a young Billy Crystal. For those not familiar with the show, Jodie was "the gay character"—one of the first (if not the first) regular gay characters on television. On one hand, I could relate to him. Even at that age (I would have been around eight years old when the show first aired), I was keenly aware of my attraction to other boys. So, to see Jodie in love with a male football player was strangely familiar—more so than seeing the hundreds of men and women getting together on *Love Boat*.

But, on the same hand, there was something very foreign to me. Basically, he was white. In fact, I didn't see any Filipino American, let alone Asian American, gay person on television or in the movies. I would tell myself, "only white men can be gay."

Where I did see Asians was in television programs and movies about war. In pretty much all the cases, we were the enemies. Or, in the case of *M*A*S*H**, we were foreigners who didn't know any better and served as comic relief to white people. I remember there was one boy who rode on my bus who would always taunt me, telling me that my parents killed his relatives. I wouldn't figure this out until later, but he had a great deal of anger within him. His grandfather died in Japan during World War II, his uncle died in Korea during the Korean War, and his father died in the Vietnam War. With Asians only portrayed as the "bad guys," it was only natural for his family and him to develop anti-Asian sentiment. Unfortunately, I didn't know any better either. There were really no Asian American role models on television, unless you count the kids on *Amazing Chan and the Chan Clan*. I remember going home and crying every afternoon, wondering why and how my own parents could murder this guy's relatives.

The taunting didn't stop at my being Asian American. I was an easy target for anti-gay epithets. In retrospect, I know that it was not because people actually thought I was gay, but because I was a sensitive, introverted, and extremely nonathletic boy. Of course, I didn't know this back then. My cousins lauded their machismo over me whenever I was forced to play some kind of sport. "Can't catch a ball, you fag?" and "Catch it, you sissy!" were phrases I became accustomed to. But, worst of all, one of my teachers actually called me a "fag" in front of my class, which caused my entire class to laugh. I knew what it meant and I learned to be careful.

In my mind, I could connect the vicious names with my burgeoning attractions to the same sex, but the root of my anxieties and insecurities probably lay in the fact that I was intersex. I was born with a condition called Klinefelter's syndrome. In the simplest terms, I was born with a different chromosomal makeup than many other boys. Whereas most boys are born with XY chromosomes and most girls are born with XX chromosomes, I was born XXY.

Of course, when I was younger I didn't know what it all meant. But I knew it meant going to the doctor a great deal and having several tests taken. I knew that it meant having to get injections of testosterone so I could complete puberty. Finally, I knew I developed differently than other boys, and that other boys my age didn't have to go through all this. It surely wasn't discussed on television—if it was, it was probably in a documentary and who watches documentaries when they're eight years old? So, in this respect, "south of normal" meant being a "freak." Normal just seemed that much farther.

In an effort to fit in, I believed I needed to sacrifice anything that would separate me from being exactly like my friends. Casting aside my ethnicity and cultural values had to be the approach. I think that many Asian Americans go through a phase where they shun their ethnic origins. For me, outside of my family, I really didn't see other Asian Americans until I was in high school. We didn't really hang out with each other. We all made sure not to form some kind of racial clique in fear of being placed on the outside. Veering off the "road to normal" would have meant we were the enemies.

My teen years were a time of cultural rebellion. I laughed at my parents who thought grades and what I studied in school were so important. This was in contrast to my white friends whose families didn't seem to mind if they got Bs and Cs. I scoffed at my parents for their connections to the Filipino American community. I was embarrassed when they spoke Tagalog in public, and I thought their connection to the Philippines was silly. Didn't they know? Didn't they watch TV? This was America. White was better. White was normal.

I wanted to be Molly Ringwald in *Sixteen Candles*—not the laughable Long Duk Dong played by Gedde Watanabe! I wanted to be part of *The Breakfast Club*!

Coming out also seemed easier to me than accepting the uniqueness of my ethnicity and race. Maybe it was because I had already established in my mind that only white men can be gay and only white men were normal. Making the connection that I subconsciously longed to be white, in a logical illogical way, my being gay made me more normal than my being Asian American.

I came out of the closet while in college. In my constant desire to fit in, I dated only white guys and went only to white gay places. I thought for sure that I'd finally found the road to normal. That is, until I started to realize that I wasn't really on the inside. Now, before I start relating these stories, I must point out that I don't think all white people are bad or malicious. I have many white friends I trust and whose company I enjoy. The point of telling these stories is to relate experiences that eventually led to my coming out as Asian American.

I remember sitting at a table with white acquaintances who started making comments about an Asian American man who entered the coffeehouse in which we were sitting. First came the comments of the exoticized Asian, likening him to a "China doll" or "geisha." Then came some stories of knowing people who've had a wonderful time exploiting sex workers in Thailand. Better yet, the comments about how they would like to "get some of that rice" made me feel as if they were bartering a commodity. Noticing my discomfort with their language, they quickly dismissed me from the stereotypes, saying, "Loren, we don't really think of you as Asian." I thought this is what I wanted, but now, instead of being the outsider looking in, "south of normal" meant the insider looking out.

At the same time, I suffered from a white boyfriend who would constantly call attention to my Asianness in negative ways. It was subtle at first, but as our relationship became more sour, my faults always seemed to be based on my race. Because I was louder and more out of the closet than he, he constantly reminded me that Asians are passive, not aggressive. At one point, he, who was angered by the fact that I was doing better than he was financially, lectured me on how Asians are ruining the economy in this country—like I have anything to do with the governments of Asian countries. I was hurtled back to my youth when I was the "enemy."

In retrospect—not that I excuse such behavior—I wonder if these men can be blamed for their feelings. The exotic Asian is consistently presented to them in lesbian, gay, bisexual, and transgender media. Although there has been some improvement, many of the images I see of Asians and Asian Americans in LGBT media are still those that are sexualized or those that are stereotyped as passive, quiet, and foreign.

After my boyfriend and I broke up, it took me a long time to get over the bitterness that led to moments of great depression. It wasn't so much the deterioration of a relationship, but the deterioration of my self-worth. Why did every step forward on the road to normal mean two steps back? In a weird way, I felt I needed to be reminded of my youth. I'm a little wiser now and understand the patterns. I have learned that many people identify as "intersex" and that Klinefelter's syndrome is not as rare as one would think (it occurs in 5 percent of men). It's sad how our society shuns gender variance and makes it difficult to talk about these issues. Boys are blue and girls are pink and never the two shall meet. My life experiences have made me appreciate how sexism, homophobia, and forms of discrimination based on gender identity go hand in hand. I have also come to learn about important intersections of race, class, gender, and sexual orientation.

So, now, when I tell people I was born "south of normal," I take it as a celebration of my diversity. Whereas I looked all my life for sameness, I find myself cherishing my otherness. The rules of normalcy are redefined and the road is no longer just an endless straight line, but one with curves and loops that make life beautiful.

I have been involved in LGBTQ communities for more than ten years now. My being weaned on the information and representations put forth by the media and understanding that power led me to GLAAD, the Gay & Lesbian Alliance Against Defamation, a national media advocacy group that promotes fair, accurate, and inclusive representation of LGBTQ communities. Where I once thought that it was the media that dictated who I was, I now realize that we have the power to turn that around. While serving as the cultural interest media manager at GLAAD, I helped GLAAD's mission by focusing on the visibility of LGBTQ people of color.

While I understand that every queer Asian American needs to find their own route on the road "south of normal," I hope that in some way, I can help create role models and decrease stereotypes so that the journey isn't so bumpy.

9

Three Masks

Kevin K. Kumashiro

I am not sure whose voices I am hearing. Are they my own? Are they the echoes of past conversations, past encounters, past exchanges that refuse to stop repeating in my head? Are they the words of youth who live only in my imagination, created as an audience for my self-debates, a beacon for times I forget why I do what I do, a symbol of all I am trying to reach? When I close my eyes, I see what appears to be me in my youth. And from my (?) mouth come these voices, but not the voices of me in my actual youth, for never in my youth did I think all these things. Or did I?

> Come out, but stay in.
> Take risks, but play it safe.
> Act now, but think first.
> Make change, but affirm oneself.

I hear the young me (?) say things that initially paralyze me with their contradiction. And each time that I search for some clarity, the young me (?) discomforts me further with even greater paradox. The voices of the young me (?) insist that I make sense of what I cannot seem to make sense of. They tell me not to close off what seems impossible; they tell me to work within that uncomfortable, foreign space of uncertainty. The young me (?) speaks against common sense. These troubling voices—they certainly did not speak for me in my youth. In a life filled with contradiction, I listened only to the voice that called for some semblance of normalcy and that offered straightforward definitions of who I was and who I was supposed to be. My own voice was one of common sense. And that was the problem.

Mask of Success

While growing up, I never really questioned who I was. I was Kevin. In some ways, I was just like anyone else. I attended an elementary school in Hawai'i where the majority of students were East Asian American (Chinese, Japanese, Korean Americans), and I never thought I looked much different from my classmates. My intermediate and high schools were not much different. East Asian Americans numbered visibly among the student body, the faculty, the administration, the community, the government, even the media. Particularly in high school, stereotypes seemed to be confirmed in many of my tracked classes. East Asian Americans dominated the college-prep classes and the honor rolls. Of course, East Asian Americans populated all tracks, as did other Asian American groups and other racial groups, but at the time I associated East Asian Americans with honors because it just seemed normal to do so.

As a middle-class Japanese American, the purpose of schooling for me was quite commonsensical. My mother was a former teacher, my father a businessman, and my older siblings had already set a precedence of good behavior, leadership, and, especially, high academic achievement. As with many of my East Asian American friends who sat in the honors classes with me, I already knew my path. And I followed it quite well. I tried to be the model student. I did my homework and whatever else it took to get the A. I shied away from activities that would get me into trouble and mix me in with the other students. I got involved in student government early and expanded to assume leadership roles in the class newspaper and school's honor society. I devoted the bulk of my time and energy to earning statewide awards in band. These were all activities dominated by East Asian Americans. So in some ways, I was just doing what I thought I was supposed to be doing. I was supposed to be a "good student." And by many accounts, I was. I do not, though, attribute my "success" only to my desire to fit the model-minority stereotype of Asian Americans. My desire to excel in school was not only a desire to conform to the stereotype that Asian Americans are smart, hard-working, and high achievers. I had many other desires.

School, after all, is not only about math and science and social studies and English. A big part of school is physical education, sports, peer culture, and popularity contests. Just as some students feel inferior in math class, or feel excluded from the culture of the science lab, or reject the official or valued knowledge and skills in English classes, or exhibit resistance to expectations in social studies classes by behaving in disruptive ways, so too did I feel inferior in athletics, and so too did I find ways to compensate for those feelings. I was not an athlete. I was not terribly coordinated. I did not have much practice throwing or catching or swinging or diving. I bore no tan from weekends at the beach. I flashed no buffed muscles when I undressed to my shorts. And perhaps most importantly, I never felt I behaved the ways boys were supposed to behave. I was quite nerdy, I was shy, I was not cool, jockish, or "masculine." And standing next to the many boys who did look and act and talk the ways I thought boys were supposed to look and act and talk, I felt ashamed, abnormal, and less-than. I do not think I realized it at the time, but subconsciously, I wanted to make up for what I felt I lacked.

To make matters worse, these very boys who intimidated me were often the ones who stirred strange feelings in me, feelings I did not know how to name. In second grade, there was a third grader who showered me with attention, and I remember feeling nervous around him while wishing we were brothers so that I could see him more often. In seventh grade, there was a classmate who used to sit by me on the bus after school, and almost daily, I remember waiting impatiently for most students to deboard so that we could exchange sexual jokes with each other. In tenth grade, during the few weeks I was seated next to the star musician in a statewide honor band, I could not stop thinking about him, and remember telling myself I was only "curious" about him, wanting to be near him yet afraid to be near him because I idolized him so. Even in college, I remember writing in my journal that a very good friend of mine was not someone I was attracted to—I just had never had such a close relationship with a male friend before. I was not gay, I told myself.

After all, I liked girls. I kissed the first girl I ever had a crush on in kindergarten. I had my first girlfriend in fifth grade, and loved exchanging little love notes. I dated girls in intermediate and high school, feeling nervous pangs in my stomach before dates, or sweaty palms when sitting in movie theaters, or mixtures of exhilaration and relief after a fun meal together. I was attracted to them, and so I could not possibly be gay. People are either straight or gay, I thought. Not until college did I find a name for my queer desires, and not until then did I come out to myself or to others as bisexual.

But my desires were stirring well before college, and as I look back to me in my youth, I start to see that a big motivation for churning out extra credit assignments to earn those As, and practicing endlessly for those music awards, and spending late nights finishing the latest edition of the newspaper or preparing for the next outing of the honor society, or even cracking one more joke during swimming class, was to compensate for parts of myself that I did not like. I could not bear to be the faggot that we all seemed to deride in our jokes and insults, or that appeared in movies only to be laughed off or killed off. And even if I could find the strength to identify as gay, I did not see myself in the predominant image of gays. Being a mahu in Hawai'i meant as much about being homosexual as about being transgender/transvestite (which I did not identify with at the time), and being gay or lesbian (forget trying to find bisexual or transgender) in the mainstream media was often reserved for white Americans. I saw no queers among my Asian American peers, or my family, or my neighbors. Being both queer and Asian American was paradoxical, if not impossible. So I was not queer. I could not be. I was convinced of that.

Today, when standards and test scores and achievement are all the buzz words in educational reform, I look to me in my youth as a reminder that the appearance of success can mask much else that goes on in the lives of our youth. Schools do not teach only academics. They are places where much else is learned, where much else is experienced, where much change takes place that often contradicts the official goals of the school. Permeating schools are stereotypes, norms, and identities that privilege some students and marginalize others; that describe who we are and prescribe who we are supposed to be; and that harm students in invisible ways. When educators and politicians are silent on these issues and fail to teach in ways that address and challenge these problems, they indirectly teach that these forms of oppression are acceptable. As valedictorian, and class officer, and honor society president, and newspaper editor, and band drum major, and winner of numerous awards, I was unquestionably a success. But, ironically, my success was merely a mask—a mask of much that was harmful when I was a student. My schooling experiences remind me that changes in education cannot address the complex, contradictory, and invisible ways that students are harmed if we continue to insist on reforms that stop at the surface and if we fail to look beyond our commonsensical views of what schools are and should be doing.

I do not need to close my eyes again to sense the young me (?) standing by my desk, watching me write. As I pause to look over, my pulse picks up and my palms tingle and start to perspire as I read a countenance of concern. With raised eyebrows, I see the young me (?) take a deep breath as he prepares to speak. Then the voices come, almost whispered, but urgently.

> Affirm self, while troubling self.
> Know others, while refusing to know.
> Learn to comfort, while desiring discomfort.
> Expand norms, while exceeding normalcy.

I do not quite get what the young me (?) is saying. I cannot quite capture the meaning of the voices. The young me (?) begins to fade away, and as I look carefully at the youth I thought I knew, I begin to question my presumptuousness of knowing. Of knowing this youth. And I begin to question my presumptuousness of telling a story about me in my youth. There is no way to tell a story that captures the whole of experience. Any story I tell is only one reading of me in my youth. Can I tell "my" story in ways that address the complexities of who I was while making explicit that, even when doing so, my story cannot help but be a partial story? Can I tell my story in ways that invite the readers of my story to reflect on different ways of reading this story and on the insights and knowledges and emotions and changes that each reading makes possible as well as impossible? As I ponder these questions, I see the young me (?) crack a smile. I thought the young me (?) had left, but I glance with relief that the translucent image lingers. And I start to realize that how I tell "my" stories is no less important than what stories I choose to tell. Paradox is both the message and the nature of these stories. There is a reason the young me (?) speaks in the way the young me (?) speaks.

Mask of Mentorship

Since elementary school, I have always wanted to be a teacher. My self-portrait, with my career goal of "Teacher," remains where it was hung years ago, in the kitchen of the house where I grew up. I am not sure why I have always felt such passion for teaching. Perhaps because my mother was a teacher. Perhaps because others told me that I had a gift for teaching. Perhaps because of the pride I felt when I could see that, through tutoring, I was helping others. Perhaps because I loved working with younger children. Perhaps because, on some level, I wanted to ensure that other children did not have to endure experiences like mine.

After attending college in California and spending some time abroad, I returned to Hawai'i to find a job as a teacher. By then, I had self-identified as bisexual for years, but had come out to very few friends, none of whom were in Hawai'i. Returning home was a return to life in the closet. I had not yet found other queers with whom I could find friendship, or support, and certainly not romance. Venturing out to find such a community came with great risks. I feared losing my friends. I feared the rejection of my family. I feared the wrath of schools that could not bear hiring a queer teacher. But I wanted to teach, and I wanted to feel that Hawai'i was still my home.

After months of searching for a job at a time when few schools were hiring, I decided to explore the possibility of teaching English in Japan. For years, I had wanted to go to Japan, the land of my ancestors. I thought I could learn about my heritage while doing what I loved most—teaching. I met with a man who headed a program that arranged such placements. He changed my life.

No one before had spoken to me as if I had already come out as queer even though I had not. No one before had made a concerted effort to reassure me that, where I wanted to go, people can find friendships and communities and activities and romantic relationships, regardless of their sexual orientation. No one before had so casually spoken of other closeted and not-so-closeted Asian/Pacific Americans, especially Japanese American men, and their experiences with homophobia in Hawai'i, with coming out while on the mainland United States, and with same-sex relationships while living in Japan. I hardly knew this man, and initially could not find the courage to accept his hinted invitation to come out, though I soon would and knew that he would be supportive when I did.

He was my first gay male mentor. He offered to lend me books by and about queer men, both fiction and nonfiction, and I accepted his offer and devoured the books when I was home alone. He offered to answer my questions about coming out, having sexual relationships, finding a community in Japan, and simply about other people like me, and over the next few months, I did ask him questions, or I hinted that I wanted to know about something but could not find the voice to ask, and he would just talk, and talk. He even offered me compliments, boosts to my uncertain self-esteem, and made me realize that the body in the mirror that for years had embarrassed me—its facial features, its thin shape, its swaying walk—was actually quite attractive to some people, including him. Perhaps most important, he did all this without making me feel uncomfortable with myself or with him. He did not pressure me to come out or to ask questions or to accept his reading materials. He did not speak constantly of sex, or continually make sexual jokes. He did not suggest that we get together socially or romantically or sexually. He did not attempt to see or touch my body. He remained a mentor, which I needed, and appreciated. I know of a number of young queer Asian/Pacific American men whose "mentors" (often older, white American, wealthier men, like mine) eventually would try to get into their pants. My mentor did not, and in that sense, I was lucky.

But today, I reread my experiences a bit differently. My mentor worked at a program connected to Japan. He was fluent in the Japanese language and knowledgeable about Japanese history and culture. He had lived and traveled extensively in Japan. He favored Japanese people and cultures over other peoples and cultures. He spoke highly of the Japanese men that he knew—their character, their values, their persona, their vulnerability, their passion, their sexual energies, their bodies. He encouraged me to view my Japanese-ness as something that made me special. He compared me constantly to another young coming-out Japanese American man, one with whom he had had sexual encounters. He slept primarily with men of Japanese descent. Not long after we had met, he went to live permanently in Japan. He clearly had a desire for things Japanese.

Although some people (of various genders and sexualities) want nothing to do with Asian Americans, others yearn for such opportunities. They desire people who fit whatever stereotypical image of Asian Americans exists in their heads: the subservient geisha, the passive houseboy, the promiscuous bar girl, the cross-dressing call boy, the multitalented tranny, and the list goes on. Or at least, they presume to know who Asian Americans are, and form relationships based on these presumptions and stereotypes. I cannot help but wonder, with whom was my mentor forming a relationship—with me, or with just another Japanese American man who fit his image of desire? Why was he interacting with me—to mentor me, or to be able to have at least some kind of interaction with me, if not sexually, then paternalistically? And now, after I realize his Japanese fetish, why do I continue to feel grateful to him? Because I had no other mentor at the time, and because I still see few mentors for young queer Asian/Pacific Americans?

In our Asian/Pacific American communities and in our queer communities, we often yearn for mentorship that is hard to find. What we often find instead are Asian/Pacific Americans who think being queer is a white disease, or queers who think being Asian is exotic, or other

queer Asian/Pacific Americans who, for a host of reasons, are unable
or unwilling to mentor. Certainly, there are many Asian/Pacific Americans who want to help the queers in their communities, and there are
many queers who want to help the Asian Pacific Americans in their
communities. However, this sometimes means being cured, or being
assimilated, or being objectified, or somehow not being taught to embrace ourselves as queer Asian/Pacific Americans. These messages
and interactions, which seem supportive and which we often call
"mentorship," fall far short of the kind of mentorship that queer
Asian/Pacific American youth deserve. Anyone can be a mentor, but
not all kinds of mentorship challenge oppression.

My understanding of myself sometimes just does not make sense. As
I write at my computer, I look up to the wall behind my desk and see a
faint image moving about, like a character on a silent movie screen, but
a fuzzy screen, and a character that changes. At first I think the character
is the young me (?), angry, flushed in the face, yelling, but mute. The
character is facing to my right, hurling hateful words at someone I cannot
yet see, someone off screen. I swear the profile of the face of the character yelling is my own face from years ago. But just when I think I know it is
a young version of me doing the yelling, the image slowly morphs into
another youth, its face indistinguishable, still angry, still clenching fists,
still yelling inaudible words. But the character doing the yelling cannot be
the young me (?) because the fuzzy movie, panning to the right, now
shows that the character is targeting the angry words to another character that looks very much like me in my youth. The same anger I once
thought flowed from the young me (?) is now what seems to bewilder
and paralyze the other young me (?) with fear and sadness. And the
movie ends. In silence. It is a very loud silence. A silence that we cannot
miss unless we choose to miss it. And yet, it is the type of silence that
seems to get ignored all the time in our lives.

Mask of Community

I did not take a job in Japan, but opted instead to remain in Hawai'i
and teach. After a few years, when I reached my mid-twenties and
was in need of finding myself and a community in which I felt I could
be me, I left Hawai'i for Wisconsin and began graduate study in education, as I had been wanting to do since my undergraduate years. In
the beginning of my first year there, I met an Asian American woman
who became one of my best friends and one of the primary reasons I
became involved in activism. Within a few months of meeting, al-

most on a whim, we decided to write a letter urging the expansion of Asian American studies on our campus. That idea ballooned into a four-year effort that involved networking with student groups, meeting with faculty and administrators, collecting signatures on petitions, contacting scholars across the country for resources and support, producing or assisting with various proposals, advising committees, organizing speakers and symposia, and participating in faculty searches. I could not and would not have done all of that alone—her energy and ideas inspired my own, and I think the reverse was true as well. We entered the world of student activism together, first working to expand Asian American studies on our campus, and eventually bringing Asian/Pacific American graduate students together for both social and academic support. Such was my entry into campus activism.

In the beginning of my first year of graduate school, I also met a queer woman who became one of my best friends, and one of the primary reasons I became involved in linking activism with my research in the field of education. Within a few months of meeting, quite by chance, she ran into me when I was carrying a book on queer issues in education. That conversation has never ended. As I turned to her time and again for advice on living out and about as queer, our conversations would inevitably connect to our growing interest in research on queer issues in education, and teaching about queer issues, and addressing queer issues in schools. She advised me on my writings and presentations, she supported me when I ran workshops for local students or educators, she nudged me when I failed to recognize my own privileges, she comforted me when the processes of coming out or finding a community or surviving academia or confronting homophobia got too overwhelming and debilitating. Now she helps me imagine ways to connect my life as an educational researcher with my life as a teacher trainer with my life as a community activist. Engaging in activism requires support. And ideas. And passion. And love. By so generously sharing these things with me, she helped make my activism possible. She continues to do so.

In my second year of graduate school, I began bridging these two parts of my life by beginning a research project on the experiences of queer Asian/Pacific American male students growing up in the United States. My research was, of course, driven largely by my personal desire to come to grips with my own racial, sexual, and gender identities and my experiences with multiple forms of oppression—identities and experiences that have always seemed fragmented and confused, yet interconnected intimately. I found a few generous folks to interview and wrote my master's thesis on their experiences with different forms of oppression, focusing on race, gender, sexual orientation, and their many intersections. My research exposed me to theories on the complex ways that oppression takes on many different forms and plays out differently in different contexts. As I was completing this project, I found myself becoming more and more determined to further complicate my thinking on oppression, and to begin to find ways to address these different forms of oppression both in schools and in society, for all people, but especially for people "like me." As I spoke with more and more people about my research, one friend suggested that I contact one of her friends, an Asian American lesbian very active in community organizing. In the summer after that second year, we met.

We had much in common, including our desire to bring queer Asian/Pacific Americans together. We each knew of a few, set a date, and soon had our first potluck dinner. Though somewhat awkward that the eight of us came together solely because we all identified as lesbian/gay/bisexual/transgender/queer and Asian/Asian American (or were the partner of someone in the room who did), I nonetheless felt strangely at ease with the group. For the first time in my life, I was in a room where almost all of us identified racially and sexually in similar ways and valued those identifications. I think others shared that feeling since we decided to form ourselves into a social organization that would meet regularly. We wanted our group, at least initially, to be only for queers of Asian descent, with non-Asian partners invited to some of our gatherings. In an attempt to be inclusive, I called our group "LGBT Asians and Asian Americans," and noted on flyers I made that we were a social and support group for lesbian, gay, bisexual, transgender, and queer Asians and Asian Americans that meets monthly. In an attempt to ensure that we remained a group for only queers of Asian descent, I also noted on the flyers that information on the times and locations of our gatherings was available by contacting me. Soon I was posting these flyers and sending out announcements via e-mail and the local newspapers. My friend and her partner usually hosted the dinners at their house. Word spread, and by the middle of that fall we had a list of more than forty people with monthly gatherings that often attracted more than twenty. We were surprised to see so many queer Asian/Pacific Americans coming out in Wisconsin, and relieved to think that our gatherings were addressing important needs in our community.

However, different people came to the gatherings for different reasons, needing different things, desiring different outcomes, and by winter, tensions were rising, and numbers slowly began to drop. People disagreed over what kind of group we should be. Some did not see connections between sexual orientation and gender identity, and were not sure why transgender folks were invited to this group. Some spoke openly about being "okay" with bisexuals, but shared their feelings that people really are one or the other and that this group, while accepting of bisexuals, should focus on gays and lesbians. Some confided in me that they preferred socializing only with men and, therefore, preferred attending the dinners when they were hosted at a man's house, or when they were certain that most of those present would be men. Some felt the gatherings were too serious or familial, and wanted gatherings of only the younger folks. Most significant, some wanted the group to be open to people of all races (or at least white men) and wanted this group to provide opportunities to find dates, especially since people attending these dinners, unlike people in bars, were certain to be open to dating people of Asian descent. At our peak, the majority of those attending the dinners were single young gay Asian (not Asian American) men.

It did not take long for my friend and me to agree that we wanted to retain our original goal of bringing queers of Asian descent together as a social and support organization, and that we did not want this to become a haven primarily for men with fetishes for Asians. We remembered the kinds of conversations we had had during our first potluck dinner, and did not want those to be replaced by a meat market. Plus, some in the group already had partners, some were women, and some made it clear that they were not interested in coming together if this was a dating group for young men. So I explained via e-mail to the members of our organization that my friend and I formed this organization with particular goals in mind, and that we wanted the group to remain one for all and only queers of Asian descent. I also explained that I felt different groups can serve different purposes, and that if people wanted to form a second group to meet the needs and wants that had been expressed, I would strongly encourage and support doing so.

I was surprised and annoyed to learn that some members continued to insist that this group should be open to single white men who are looking to date Asian men. They did not seem to understand why they could not bring their non-Asian gay male acquaintances with them or why I would get upset when they did. One member even informed me that some of the white men and even some of the Asian men who had been to the dinners said that I "oppressed white people" because I wanted a group exclusively for people of Asian descent.

My initial anger eventually turned to sadness and regret as I realized that the tensions in our group could have sparked discussions about identity and community. In particular, the tensions over the social aspect (or lack thereof) of this group could have invited conversations about, say, racism, sexism, ageism, and other forms of oppression within queer communities and different ways to address them. But no, I had initially become so caught up in trying to defend the original goals of the group that I failed to take advantage of this opportunity to complicate as well as strengthen our senses of identity and belonging.

Further, I failed to be the kind of mentor of which I just argued we need more. Early in the group's formation, I remember telling a friend that a number of the younger men in the group seem to like talking to me about my life or simply asking advice about their own, and while I was flattered that they seemed to view me as a mentor, I was quickly finding myself drained by the amount of time and energy I spent on the phone, over lunch, in small groups, and so forth. I remember saying I felt annoyed (and then guilty for feeling annoyed . . .) that in a group I helped to form as a way to find support for myself, I ended up serving primarily as a source of support for others. I wasn't finding the balance for myself. And rather than trying to find additional ways to meet the needs and desires of others in the group— especially my new younger friends—I pulled away from my mentoring role, and eventually, from the leadership of the group.

Ironically, by trying to protect the group, by closing off discussion of what I saw as oppressive movements by some in the group, and by trying to prevent my becoming overwhelmed as the group's leader, I saw many in the group leave, and thus, saw many of us lose out on what the group could have offered. Our competing visions of what constitutes a community actually made strengthening "our" community quite difficult. I am not saying that because we were all queers of

Asian descent we "belonged" together. But I am saying that the group let slip away an opportunity to engage in activist movement when we all thought we were doing exactly that.

Today, I continue to wrestle with notions of what it means to organize for queer Asian/Pacific Americans. I created an e-mail discussion list for queer Asian/Pacific Americans across the country to engage in conversations on activism and social change. Eventually, I had hoped it would serve as a primary means of connecting, building on one another's work, and envisioning collaborative efforts to address multiple forms of oppression in our lives, such as with a national organization or network. But as with any effort, this online community has its strengths and weaknesses. This is not surprising, since different people prioritize different needs, feel different desires, work in different circumstances, and relate in different ways. There are many barriers to coming together and working together. I remind myself that activism is a complex, always shifting, never ending process, and that attempts to bring about change can, ironically, exclude the very people we are trying to reach. As we look to the future, we should keep these tensions in mind.

10

All-American Asian

David C. Lee

Mom caught me one morning removing one of her hair curlers from my head. "Ayaah!" she cried, as she stood there looking bemused. "Oh, hi, Ma," I said, nervously yanking the curler out of my hair. "I just, I just, wanted to . . . um." "It's okay to try to improve your looks, son," she affirmed mercifully. Her bemusement waned as her bespectacled eyes moved from my bobbing hair to my face. "But remember, no matter what you do, you'll always be Chinese." I blushed as I looked in the mirror, trying to flatten out the curled hump on my head. At age thirteen, a boy starts to notice how he looks; he wants to be cool. And I admired that soft wavy hair, brightened with golden highlights that my school friend James had. He was broad-shouldered; shirts hung on him just right. Occasionally during playful moments I'd take liberties, brushing my fingertips over the glistening blond hairs on his arms. I felt plain next to him. We compared TV characters. I told James he was James, James Bond, and he'd laughingly say that I was Sing, Hop Sing. I would laugh too, but only to please James.

I had come out to my mother two years earlier. Mom . . . I dream of men, strong, handsome, muscular white men, the ones on TV, romance books, and magazine covers. They make love to me, press themselves against me, and kiss me with tongues wet. Waves of tension and emotion would rise, and a falling feeling pulls from the pit of my stomach. A warm wetness gently awakens me, and I think of James and his wavy blond hair until I fall back asleep. Mom stayed composed and said, "This means that you can make a woman pregnant." She then touched my hand reassuringly and whispered, "The interest in men is just a phase," nodding as if she knew. But the phase lasted and Mom whined continually, "You're such a nice, smart boy.

Why can't you give up that gay stuff and marry a Chinese woman?"
She waited for my response, as if I would just say, "Sure, okay, Mom.
I'll do it."

Dad died. I was the first-born son and that meant I was obligated to
be the head of the household. Pressure. I didn't want to be the first-
born son. I didn't want to marry a Chinese girl. And I didn't want to
take care of my family anymore. Shit, I gave Mom and Dad my childhood. I worked for the family business, baby-sat my siblings, and
gave up an adolescent social life for them. Unlike my school peers, I
had to earn my As studying during odd hours, after bedtime. I'd miss
the last cinema show. Life was hell.

Living in Arizona, I was teased at school for being Asian, and I
was teased at home for being gay. I was a sissy for being too sensitive,
too sensitive for protesting being called sissy, and a "big mouth" for
being too articulate. The white kids in school went on vacations with
their family. They wore cool clothes. They didn't have to eat that
bittermelon crap. Their parents spoke "normal" English. Dad and
Mom pronounced "LA," "elway," and "oil," "oyo," for Christ's sake.
To a seventeen year old living in Arizona being Chinese was not cool.
Although mocking my Chinese language, mimicking Chinese accents, and branding me a foreigner didn't kill me, I'm not sure how
much stronger it had made me. Twenty years later, racial denigration
still makes me ill. Each time it happens, a lifetime flashes before me,
and memories of all that hatred haunt me. I remember I was twelve
years old when Dad was driving on the highway and a group of teenage white guys drove up next to us. They gave Dad a loathsome glare,
pulled their eyes back to mimic our eyes, and stuck their middle fin-
gers at us, laughing. What did their parents teach them? Why? I tried
to ignore them—a typical Asian survival response. But Dad returned
their gesture. He gave the finger back, but in a timid, hesitant manner
that humiliated me. Ignoring them was far better than retaliating fee-
bly, I thought. "Why did you do that!" I yelled. "Oh, shut up!" Dad
·crackled, pushing up his black-rimmed glasses. His face turned red,
as his head leaned toward the steering wheel. I sat back, feeling
ashamed and defeated, and thinking what a drag it was to be Chinese.
How helpless we were. But I felt sorry for Dad, too. He didn't ask for
this. Looking back now, I'm glad Dad gave them the finger.

In college I tried to color my hair blond. Black roots had to be cov-
ered every two weeks. I used drabber to tone down the stubborn or-

ange tints that appeared when naturally dark hair is overlightened. I didn't mind because it made me feel less Chinese, and I liked that feeling. Never mind what Mom had told me. With my big round eyes and olive complexion, the hair color made me look like a Hispanic with bleached hair. That was okay. I became deluded, believing that racist comments weren't so hurtful because they didn't pertain to me. The orange-blond hair separated me from that class of laughable Asians. Even if I was seen as Chinese, I felt "cool," with the over-processed hair and all. And for a couple of years, I forgot that I was Chinese.

After college I moved to San Francisco, mainly to be gay and to find for myself that boyfriend I had always wanted. He was going to be handsome, athletic, and white, just like the ones in the movies, or on the covers of gay magazines and *Advocate* escort ads. I was told that I was handsome often enough to believe that I could actually date men like that. But instead, with few exceptions, I attracted mainly the "rice queens." Rice queens are typically older, nonathletic, and somewhat "cultured" gay white men who have distinct tastes for Asians, particularly the smooth, lean, boyish-looking ones. But I wanted someone my own age, not someone who exoticized me. I wanted James. After a few months in San Francisco, it dawned on me that white men generally desired only other white men. Actually, it seemed *everyone* desired white men. Asians were invisible, and the invisibility hurt like a racial slur.

In San Francisco I learned the protocols of gay culture. Asian men competed with one another for their white prize, the rice queen or the occasional white boy who happened to find Asians attractive too. But Asian men would never date each other. It would be like dating one's sister. Ugh. Besides, we've learned that attractive men don't look like us. Attractive and desirable men are white, not Asian. So rather than be white (as we can't), Asian men date white men, or at least we try. The higher status we put on white men makes their affirmation highly sought after. If we could have a white man love us, we would become almost better than Asians, better than ourselves. We want to hear them tell us how beautiful we are, and their affirmation becomes an addiction. Am I the most beautiful Asian man you've been with? Am I more beautiful than that Asian guy over there, and over there? Well, when is the white man's affirmation enough?

In the media, we're the sexless Hop Sing from *Bonanza*—the Chinese cook with buckteeth and a caricaturized Asian accent. We're the screaming kung fu master who gets his butt kicked by the white man. We're the follower, the half-witted sidekick (Jackie Chan—you better fight back!). We're the nerdy Asian foreign exchange student who never gets a date. We're the scrawny, queeny, effeminate guy who likes to work in clothing retail and squeal at discount tags. We only look good when we're hyper-feminized in haute couture drag. Older white men are our sugar daddies. And the white man's affirmation will never be enough. Perhaps because we really don't like what he's affirming. So why don't we start affirming ourselves, on our own terms?

I stopped coloring my hair by age twenty-one, and it became naturally black again. What is the "American" standard of beauty anyway? And how do people of color fit in? Who made up these standards? I cringe at comments such as "Oh, he's a blond, blue-eyed, all-American type." It's outrageously ignorant. Damn it, I am an "all American." I'm a black-haired and brown-eyed all-American man, thank you very much. My genetic make-up precludes me from your white standards of beauty. Shame on you for imposing them on me. Shame on you for your arrogance. The truth is, Asians are HOT! Asian men *are* sexy, dateable, and very delectable. I say to all Asians, let's stop hiding from one another like secret enemies. Let's talk to one another, share our pains, insecurities, and let's affirm ourselves. Let one another know how beautiful we are. More important, let's stop being just one another's damned "sister," and let's go out!

In the 1980s, while I was riding in a crowded Muni bus along upper Market near Castro Street in San Francisco, a young, shy-looking Asian man, thinly built and wearing torn tennis shoes, squeezed in and was literally shoved by the crowd against a taller white gay man, whom I had noticed earlier when I got on. His eyes were cold blue, and he had platinum blond hair, cropped close to his head. I saw his frown beneath his Castro-clone mustache. He'd been in the gay clubs I went to, but he had never acknowledged me. As the Asian guy moved up against him, he shoved the Asian man away. "Don't lean on me, you!" Silent and wide-eyed with horror, the Asian man tried to leap away. He wouldn't look back at the white man. "You probably don't even speak English!" he said with disdain. The Asian man's lips pressed shut tightly, his nostrils pulsating. He glanced at me for a moment. I nodded to him to acknowledge what had just happened, and he managed a smile back at me. Then he looked down as if the indignity had sunk in again. In these situations, I would have normally felt shame for the foreigner, wishing he would speak better English and fight back with articulate force, wishing he wouldn't be such an effete minority. But this time I felt shame for the white man.

Having lived a lifetime of self-denigration for being Asian, I realized at that moment how tired I was from it all. As I watched my fellow Asian man, I asked myself, "So what if he didn't speak English? Why is that so shameful? Why did the white man hate us so much? Why do we hate ourselves so much!" I felt a surge of emotion swell within me as I watched him shake his head in disgust at the Asian guy. Then I noticed the Asian guy, in his tense silence. I felt sad for him. I turned and looked up at the white man. "Excuse me, this is a crowded bus, and you didn't have to be rude to him," I snapped, pointing to the Asian man. The white guy snarled at me, "What, are you his fucking brother?" People put their newspapers down and it seemed as though all eyes were on me. "He's not my brother." I paused for a second looking down, searching for my response. With a little more gumption I looked at him again, "And what is it to you whether or not he speaks English?" "Go fuck yourself! Fucking Jap," he scoffed with a more apparent frown. Strangely, the weight of his caustic lashing didn't hit me. Rather, I was amused by how poor his diction was. His pallor began to change to a moderate crimson. I loosened my tie to continue, "He has every right to be here as you do. And God Bless America to you too, you racist . . . you redneck!" As if God was watching, my stop came up, the bus door bolted opened, and I jumped out before the man could retort. Cool summer drizzle sprayed my face as my heart pounded. My body shook. Resentment began to seep inside me for speaking my mind, like a virus breaking through my skin. But an inner voice came through. "David, don't ever apologize for being Asian. You're no less important than that white man, and neither is the other Asian man." What gall he had to demean us for not knowing English, for being Chinese! Christ, first these white guys ignore us because we are Asian, and then they disparage us for being Asian. And even more insulting is that we continue to seek their favor. I mean, something is seriously wrong with this picture.

I went home that day darkened with anger. I told my partner about the incident. I told him I was fed up with feeling like a second-class citizen. I wasn't going to hate myself anymore for being Asian. I told him I shall no longer defer to any white man's entitlement. Because today I saw an Asian man's dignity and entitlement robbed by a white man. And it was hideous. I told my partner that I made the white man give it back. Self-satisfied after reporting the account, I waited for my partner's response. He shook his blond head, gave that condescending smirk of his and said, "Oh God, you've become one of those angry militant minorities." He further accused me of playing the racial victim and scolded me for jumping all over the white guy for something that I wasn't even a part of. "But I was a part of it!" I cried. "It's not just about a guy being rude to another guy. It's about a white guy being rude to an Asian guy based on his race." I turned my back to him and snapped, "I'm sick of it!" With a patronizing smirk, he retorted in cool analytical discourse, "Well the Japanese are the worst racists, if you want to talk about racism . . . World War II [blah blah blah] and the Chinese word for white people is 'white ghost' [blah blah], you should have just minded your own business." I rolled my eyes and thought, "How typical." I wanted my partner to be angry and indignant with me. I wanted him to be my ally. But he was so smug. And I stupidly deferred to him. This time my self-identity was screaming at me. My ancestors were kicking me in the stomach, and I couldn't sleep. Eventually I grew intolerant of his patronizing pats on my head, his condescending corrections of my speech, his ignoring my consideration in major decisions, and his treating his friends better than he did me. He became no longer my golden boy, and I promised myself to love an ally next time.

Meet a guy who agrees to be your ally against racism. And I don't mean the liberal progressive gent who showers you with words of racial support and understanding but disappears when supportive action is needed. When it's time to stand up against his fellow white man for being racist, where is he? When it's time to protest aloud, why is he silent? Didn't notice? Wasn't aware? Why didn't he notice? Why wasn't he aware? He has ample opportunities in restaurants, bars, clubs, grocery stores, doctor's offices, the work environment, home, with friends, relatives, and cohorts. Notice who gets served first. Notice who gets asked, "How is everything?" Notice who gets more eye contact. Who gets more attention, credit, and credibility?

Who gets the promotion? It's usually the white guy. Oh, and notice who's invisible too. He's used to his entitlement. That's white privilege. He's used to not having to notice. And when you point it out to him, don't let him act surprised and make excuses for anyone. Don't let him say you're too sensitive and you shouldn't have even said anything. Don't let him ever accuse you of white bashing. And don't let him make you doubt yourself. Why? Because the liberal white companion gets to enjoy his meal and service when you don't. Have him earn your love by giving you sixty minutes of justice a day. Have him be in your shoes and fight your racial battles while you enjoy your dinner. *Bon appétit.*

We as people of color must broadcast our narratives. We must speak out for ourselves because we will be disappointed if we always rely on others to speak for us. Our narratives make us visible. We can only hope that white people will listen, believe us, and act. Dining out with my white friend, I often pointed out to him how he was usually the one served first, how the server tended to give him more attention, and how I was usually ignored. He didn't believe me at first. He thought it was just a coincidence, that I was just exaggerating. But I piqued his awareness and he started to see what I meant. Whereas before he was blind, now he could acknowledge my narrative.

I asked the waiter what the special was for the day and he answered my white friend. A litany of similar themes accumulated. I told my friend that I never wanted to eat at this restaurant again. He took my hand and said he was sorry. Without saying more, he flagged the manager down and complained. He told the staff that he was offended, that they had been ignoring me, and that the staff should have diversity training. My friend charged that the staff paid attention to him because he was white. The staff was defensive in response to the accusation, "We didn't notice. We don't discriminate. We didn't mean to." But intentions are worthless when accusations are true. We're already hurt. For once, a white person called them on it. I felt great relief from his gesture. I thought, "What a cool guy! He honored me! He's my hero!" But he was an ally only for that day. Will he speak up for me tomorrow? The next day? And the next? People of color cannot fight racism alone. We need allies. It's an ongoing fight, and it's not only our fight—it's everyone's.

One of the reasons that racism is so difficult for people of color to talk about is that white people usually deny responsibility for it. They blame the victim—we're too sensitive, too illiterate, too submissive, too angry, and too short! Racism is analyzed away and we're left with our invalidated experiences. But if we continue to share our experiences and our narratives, we will be heard, and I believe action will happen. Actually, we don't have much choice. Recent polls tell us that the "model minority" is a lie. Asians are far less trusted and liked than any other minority in this country. Surprised? I have given countless workshops to various educational, business, and other groups small and large across this country on issues of racial diversity, and in my diversity work we teach that the truth in our shared experiences can break through the fear and hatred behind racism. Our personal narratives have power. In turn, we also learn that white people need support in exploring what it really means to be white and what white privilege really is. How can they build alliances with people of color and not fear retaliation or rejection? And how can we as queer people of color heal from our lifetime of internalized racism, homophobia, and shame for being who we are? It's especially difficult in the queer community where white supremacy is so entrenched. I'm not talking about the Ku Klux Klan here, but it's the same effect. White male bodies are sprawled across magazines, tabloids, billboards, gay TV, movies, and gay clubs. Asians are rendered invisible in the gay community—and yeah, it's like a racial slur. The fight against racism and homophobia is a difficult journey for all people and we cannot prevail without each others' mutual support and understanding, our personal narratives, and compassion for each other. Just remember, no matter what you do, you can't escape who you truly are.

11

Queerly a Good Friday

Jeanette Mei Gim Lee

As a clergy candidate in the queer Christian denomination, the Universal Fellowship of Metropolitan Community Churches, I work to uphold Christian traditions in ways that are responsive to the plurality of backgrounds in our community, as I did this year when commemorating Holy Week. Without having had the influence of institutional religion in my childhood, and having lived the majority of my life in the San Francisco Bay Area, demographically the region with the least amount of regular church attendance in the country, Holy Week is unfamiliar terrain for me. Yet, as a biracial lesbian and self-identified queer who entered ministry in her early twenties, my immersion into the unfamiliar is, paradoxically, familiar.

In seminary, I've been trained to interpret the Bible with a "critical hermeneutic." As someone who did not grow up cuddling the Bible at bedtime, but rather experienced the Bible as an arsenal for hate, I've wrestled with its volatile social, political, ideological, religious, and spiritual value. Conservative Christianity asserts that the Bible determines what God wills and how Christians should live. I am opposed to imbuing the Bible with such a degree of authority over moral doctrines and law. Furthermore, I am opposed to ecclesiastical hierarchy dictating how the Bible governs my experiences. Instead, I believe the Bible's messages to be formative, existential, and inspirational, that is, open to different interpretations and responses that are informed by our different life experiences. I acknowledge that the Bible has already come to be influential and pervasive in U.S. culture, ideology, and aesthetics. But there is much more to learn from the Bible. The Bible can have value in helping discern what God is saying or doing *right now*.

Poised for social justice ministry as a queer of color, I feel called on to expose the complexities, intersections, and mechanisms of racial and sexual oppressions and power disparities. My wielding the Bible, of all things, may appear as if I wish to bang my head against the walls of cathedrals of oppression. However, having experienced oppression, I find in the Bible fertile grounds for deconstructing and strategically "taking back the word" while finding new ways to work toward God's peace, justice, and liberation. Doing so, I believe, requires reading the Bible as a "vein into the vessel" of dominant hegemony, that is, as a means to disrupt the prevailing, oppressive discourses in society. The goal is to provide a proactive discourse that does not cooperate with readings that only apologetically disrupt hegemony. The goal is not, for example, to interpret the Bible by trying to prove to dominant groups that queers of color are just like them (which is really just a manifestation of internalized oppression), or to use methodologically valid academic analyses to try to convince conservatives that their homophobic readings of scripture are fallacious (which often only expends energy). Personally, as I aim toward liberation I proactively reflect on *my* queer-of-color experience in light of the Bible.

My approach is informed by liberation theology, wherein activism and spirituality are one and the same. Praying with my brain has the same merit as praying with my hands and feet while marching in protest, organizing, and speaking up for the marginalized. I feel the presence of God when I am working for justice. Working for justice is how I pray. Of course, my most meaningful prayer/activism is when I can address the intersections of race and sexuality.

This year, on Good Friday, our San Francisco congregation observed the Stations of the Cross. I was asked to present on the event in the Passion narrative in which Simon carried the battered Jesus' cross to the crucifixion site. In our worship liturgy, Simon aided Jesus' stumble toward his death by helping him stand up, wiping away his sweat, and carrying the heavy cross. As usual, I stumbled to appropriate this text with authentic personal significance and activist implications. In my exegetical research I discovered that Simon appears in Matthew 27:31-32 (NRSV):

> After mocking [Jesus], they stripped him of the robe and put his own clothes on him. Then they led him away to crucify him. As

they went out, they came upon a man from Cyrene named Simon; they compelled this man to carry his cross.

Simon's origin from Cyrene indicates that he was a nonnative, an immigrant. The only other time in the New Testament where Cyrene is mentioned is in reference to the coming of the Holy Spirit in Acts 2:3-12, where those who spoke a plethora of languages found themselves able to communicate:

> Divided tongues, as of fire, appeared among them, and a tongue rested on each of them. All of them were filled with the Holy Spirit and began to speak in other languages. . . . And at this sound the crowd gathered and was bewildered, because each one heard them speaking in the native language of each . . . speaking about God's deeds and power. All were amazed and perplexed, saying to one another, "What does this mean?" (NRSV)

On a queer commemoration of Good Friday at the Metropolitan Community Church in San Francisco, I presented the following personal, bicultural proactive reading.

* * *

For weeks during middle school I slept on the couch. Grandma/ Barbara Lee/Chan Sien Kim's health wasn't so good. She complained of being lonely. Her barely passable English no longer enabled her to check out groceries. Once she even fell down the stairs. She would sit on the sofa all day watching game shows. Whenever I gave her an ear, she would dig into her cardigan sweater pockets, give me a starlight mint with Kleenex dust on the wrapper, and lament that she could no longer work. Sometimes she'd begin to tell me a story about her past, then midway through toss her wrists, as if swatting a fly, frustrated by her incomplete English. Or was it my incompetent Cantonese? Sometimes I would catch her staring out the window with slumped shoulders watching my dad doing yard work, the sun reflecting off her bifocals. Looking lost in the glare of her lens, her bony face looked fragile, sad. Her wrinkled skin seemed carved by all the borders and customs crossed.

Grandma, who had lost her husband, or gained her freedom, ten years before, always complained of being lonely. She complained that my sister and I were "too American," didn't go to church enough, didn't go to Chinese school, played too much "ball," and ate sweets before dinner. However, she never vocalized what I believed was her preeminent disgruntlement: life on the borderlands.

These were tension-filled weeks. Mom and Dad didn't talk to each other jovially at dinner anymore. My siblings and I knew better than to ask when we'd get our bedroom back, when we'd get to eat tacos instead of bittermelon and lotus root soup, or when we'd be allowed to let our dog, whose presence my grandmother resented and considered absurdly ridiculous, sit on the couch with us while we watched reruns of *Happy Days*.

For my old-country grandma, an "old folks" home meant abandonment. Inherent in her arranged marriage to an eldest son was the expectation that she dutifully toil after her mentally ill mother-in-law the majority of her sacrificed young adult years. I can envision her rubbing Tiger Balm into my great-grandmother's back. In a motion like peeling a carrot, with a spoon she would be scraping a Chinese-like character up and down her spine and to-and-fro her shoulder blades to heal a disease.

Now her turn, my mother, an "American"—which to many of us meant the same as "white"—was going to have none of it. After a series of nights of thundering fists and ricocheting yells, my dad found a live-in caretaker. Diane X spent two weeks with my grandmother at her house, shopping, cooking, and cleaning for her. "Too messy and cooks too salty," my grandmother judged. Then, Jane Y spent one week with my grandmother. "She took money out of purse!" my grandmother charged. Then, Betty Z spent a month with my grandmother. "She from Shanghai. Stuck up," my grandmother dismissed. In the next sentence she whispered into my ear, "I live with you; we have fun together," just as I noticed my dog in the backyard looking longingly at the door to be let in.

Next came Mei Gim. My white mother called her My Gum; my father never corrected her. Then again, neither did Mei Gim. She came into my grandmother's life at the critical juncture. My father—his mother's child, and a mother to the child his mother had become—had laid it down: "Last chance or to the Senior Home you go."

Throughout his life, it was his inherited duty to be the translator of "America" to her.

Mei Gim was scattered. She had no consciousness of "American" customs. She belched at dinner, wore cotton sweat pants and silk blouses, and used nylon leggings to compress her hair like a nightcap. I immediately liked her. Grandma said, "She knows how to clean, but cooks with too much oil," and it was a go! The muting fog lifted at home, I could chase my dog up and down on the couch cushions, and my parents' mouths ran convivially back and forth.

For years I visited Mei Gim and Grandma. My grandma became Mei Gim's translator of "America" and month by month Mei Gim greeted me with more and more English acquired from adult night school and from *Days of Our Lives.* Mei Gim would brave car-sickness and take me out to lunch often with a notebook and pen as our mediator. I discovered her husband was abusive and moving here kept her away from him. She'd puzzle about the fuss we made at Thanksgiving and would sit next to my grandmother, filling her plate watchfully, and then, over my parents' objections, stubbornly wash the dishes. She and my grandmother walked to the local park daily for exercise. They were often sighted giggling together like schoolgirls. She massaged my grandmother's arthritic back. She gave my grand-mother water when she was thirsty and dry. She *was* the water to my family's journey through the barren terrain of compromising cul-tures.

On the morning the local hospice arranged the bed and morphine that would take my grandma to the World of Yin, I sat with Mei Gim. At the kitchen/mah-jongg table, Mei Gim spread butter on her toast, scraping the coarseness with a squealing knife. Emotionally raw, I thanked her for being the salve for my family. She said, "Your grand-mother, my mother," then looking in my eyes, "You smart; you grandma proud of you. You learn; you stay in school. You meet *good* man; you get married."

When my father and I removed the life support tube from my grandmother's parched mouth, Mei Gim wailed, stroking her sweaty forehead, and later applied lipstick on my grandmother before the coroner's men carried her body out of the house.

Mei Gim, whose last name I still don't know, allied many worlds—hers, my grandmother's, my father's, my mother's, and my own. I see

Mei Gim now and then. With riveting determination, she always re-members to insist that I get married. But, my back is *not* a bridge to cultural "tradition." I want to be a welder, with a bandanna for sweat, like Rosie.

12

Three Strikes, I'M OUT!
A Chicana Samoan Dyke's Tale

Cristina M. Misa

The morning is here . . . Another day in the neighborhood . . .
Another day to breathe and be grateful . . . My goddess made
sure I lived to see another day . . .

Three blocks west of I-15, 125th and El Camino.

Folks are always going somewhere fast on the freeway, but they
never exit. Folks exit on 124th or 126th, but never on my street. Why?
I wondered. I guess those folks were afraid of what they would see.

My street looked like all the rest. Tall and dead-looking palm trees,
broken fences surrounding large apartment complexes, and kids . . .
lots of kids on the streets chillin', playing ball, or smoking out. There
was always something going on.

Come to think about it, I remember huge trees that blocked the
sight of those who passed on the I-15. Those trees seemed to separate
us from the rest of the world, preventing others from ever knowing
what went on beyond those trees.

Not that the local TV news stations didn't report daily on the conditions of my neighborhood. "This place called 'the jungle' by residents has tragically taken an innocent life in yet another night of gang
violence," said one reporter.

Why didn't anybody ever look past those trees and the many news
reports to see the madness? Couldn't they see that the violence in my
neighborhood wasn't just in the streets? Couldn't they see that the
hate that existed wasn't just between rival gang members? I ask,
couldn't they just see me?

"Bitch . . . you better choose. Are you with us or them? We ain't gonna have no traitors in our family, I don't care if you're a wetback!" yelled Junior.

"Fuck you, puto! Who ya calling wetback? Your family came here by boat. Cristina won't choose ya'll Samoans over La Raza. She'll run with us! Her loyalty is with us," yelled Chuy.

They tell me to choose, but do I really have a choice? My blood . . . my family. . . . Vicious, hateful words keep flying. No one talks about being biracial in rival family territories. Why is it that I must be forced to negotiate between two marginalized communities in which both experience daily acts of racism, xenophobia, and classism? More important, why should I have to choose between two racial identities when I am BOTH?

Living in a constant state of negotiation between my Samoan and Mexican families, I came to understand being biracial as having identities to *respect* and *own* rather than having to show loyalty toward only one.

STRIKE ONE.

"I like to call this meeting to order. It's nine o'clock, March twenty-first. We need to talk about the conference. It's takin' place in less than two months. We only have the workshops confirmed. Martín is passing out the list. I think everyone will be happy with the results," said Rogelio.

Chicano Politics, Chicano History, El Movimiento Chicano, Chicanas in El Movimiento . . .

More than thirty workshops, but they all pretty much sounded the same. Only *one* workshop out of a three-day conference addressed *anything* dealing with gender, women, and/or sexual identity. There were twenty-five proposals for gender and sexuality workshops dealing with the areas of relationships, AIDS and homophobia, Chicana Herstory, and sex/sexual identity . . . *and only one was chosen?*

This conference was to serve as a place to become educated and liberated as a *movement* of the Chicano people. But the Chicano people only meant Chicano men. The voices of others were silenced. It didn't matter if the voices were of Chicanas, Chicana/o queers, or those Chicanas/Chicanos who were bi/multiracial. What hurt most is that the men of the conference were not the only ones with this attitude.

"Damn, look at her, that bitch is going to throw out that women-power shit again. Who does she think she is . . . queen Chicana? The baddest loca in Aztlán. All that feminist shit is only for white bitches, not for Chicano women," said Lola.

"That bitch has fuckin' better choose . . . is ella a Chicano woman or a Chiiicaana? For her sake and if she wants a fine Chicano brother to fuck, she better know what to choose," mocked Adela.

"Mira, she's going to the bathroom. Someone needs to go beat her down. Her feminist shit is fuckin' up my game. If Rogelio gets pissed tonight, there is no way I am getting some," said another.

Why do I still need to defend the power of *La Mujer* in the face of my own "sisters"?

Being an organizer for a variety of Chicana/o and other student of color conferences and organizations, my level of consciousness as a feminist has grown to a point at which I no longer accept the oppressive conditions men or women put on me. In the process of doing so, I have learned that as a Chicana feminist who deviates from the nationalist politics of my "brothers and sisters," I will be attacked when I am fighting for the very *liberation* they all preach.

STRIKE TWO.

"Let's go to lunch, Ma," I shouted.

"OK, mi'ja, but nothing too expensive. I want to make sure we have enough to buy you some nice things, maybe even a . . . a . . . umm," Mom said hesitantly.

"Buy what, Ma?" I asked.

"A . . . a dress," Mom quickly said. "Honey, you need to look more feminine. How will you ever get a boyfriend?"

"What da you mean? Do you think a dress is really going to make the difference in a MAN liking me? Whatever, Ma. I just wish you get over trying to marry me off."

"I know, mi'ja, but I would like to see you happy. I only want the best for my daughters, nothing more. Besides, my angel deserves the best."

My mommy's angel has just broken the halo . . . . No longer would I live her lie . . .

At our favorite restaurant in Westville, my mom, overwhelmed with tears, saw *La Virgen*. I was no longer the same daughter she raised, who would be married in a big church and have her beautifully mixed grandchildren. I was now a disgrace.

Before she turned away and left me at the restaurant she cried out, "How can you do this to the family . . . how can you do this to yourself? What will the rest of the family think? You know those Samoan grandparents of yours will never accept this! And as a Catholic, neither will I, EVER! *Ay Díos,* what did I do wrong? God says you are a sinner and you will pay one day for your sins!"

My world collapsed for a moment, and then . . .

I remembered the beautiful woman I had waiting at home.

She's the reason I believe in love.

STRIKE THREE.

Being queer, biracial, and a feminist (or as I identify: a woman who actively works toward "letting people have it" for their multiple levels of ignorance and hate) in a world that silences, threatens, and incarcerates those who are different, I felt the *three strikes initiative* was perfect for describing *my place*. Most know the three strikes initiative as a legal way to unjustly imprison poor men and women of color for life. In the act of disrupting this horrifying legal practice of three strikes, I have chosen to present each of these strikes in a different way. For me each strike now represents . . .

> My strike of pride: I challenge family loyalties for being Mexican and Samoan.

> My strike of resistance: I challenge sexist and homophobic practices as a woman in sexist Chicano organizations.

> My strike of liberation: I challenge the heterosexual life that my family members, friends, and fellow activists have expected me to live.

In essence, it is with each of these strikes that I now

> . . . challenge multiple notions of ignorance
> . . . disrupt multiple levels of comfort
> . . . create a safe and consistent space

. . . for all queers of color to take up the struggle against racist, homophobic, sexist, xenophobic, and essentializing practices and beliefs

experienced within the confines of our educational institutions, political organizations, and even *our own families.*
You still ask why this is important to understand?

No progressive movement can succeed while any member of the population remains in submission.

Cherríe Moraga
The Last Generation

Need I say any more?

13

Activism and the Consciousness of Difference

Pauline Park

My childhood was marked above all by difference. My brother and I were the only nonwhite children in our elementary school, an otherwise all-white public school on the south side of Milwaukee. We were the only Asians, the only adoptees, and the only twins in our class. As the only Korean adoptees, we were the only children with parents of a different race and ethnicity. We were the only kids in our class born in a foreign country. We were also the only kids who knew all the capitals of all fifty states; that alone marked us as the hyper-intellectuals of our class. We were also the only targets of abuse every December 7, as other (usually older) kids would invariably shout anti-Japanese slogans, though even at that young age, I knew that it was completely illogical to hold a pair of Korean adoptees responsible for the Japanese attack on Pearl Harbor.

Although I cannot know whether this is true, I suspect that I was the only boy in my school who had recurring dreams of being alone in the ladies' department in a department store, free to try on all the women's clothes in the store. I knew that I was transgendered at the age of four, long before I had even heard the word. The very first week of school, I saw girls wearing stretch pants with stirrups, and decided that I wanted a pair. But my mother's shocked reaction at the suggestion that she buy me a pair was my introduction to the sex/gender binary. Puberty brought strange and inexplicable attractions to other boys, and at sixteen I came to self-identify as gay. Growing up in an evangelical Protestant household with devoutly Lutheran parents and grandparents, I realized instinctively that I could not be who I truly was until I reached adulthood, and I waited more or less patiently for

it to come. Going away to college brought liberation from the constraints of family and childhood. My very first semester, I came out as
gay, realizing even then that gay male identity could not fully encom-
pass the reality of who I was. But as liberal as Madison was in the late
1970s—it had been ballyhooed as the "radical Mecca of the Midwest" in the 1960s, Wisconsin's answer to Berkeley—there was no
recognition at the time of transgender identity in the lesbian and gay
community, much less a support system for openly transgendered
people. So the process of actualizing an identity as an openly transgendered woman would take many more years.

The difference that marked me from the very beginning—as a
foreign-born Korean adoptee, an intellectually curious child, a male
attracted to other males, and a male with a feminine gender identity—
were all factors shaping my identity that would eventually help shape
my activism years later. Wordsworth wrote, "the child is father to the
man." In my case, the boy was father to the woman. My involvement
with lesbian, gay, bisexual, transgender (LGBT) communities has not
lessened my consciousness of difference but rather heightened it. Just
as in childhood, I am invariably "the other" in any group that I'm in,
whether it be the only transgendered woman or the only Asian in an
LGBT organization, the only LGBT/queer person in an Asian American organization, or the only adoptee in an API group. However, in an
age of identity politics, such difference is not necessarily a bad thing,
and instead can be used to enhance inclusivity and diversity.

For example, in January 1997, when I joined with several others to
found a community center in the borough of Queens, New York, my
presence as the only transgendered person prompted those present to
reconsider "Queens Lesbian and Gay Community Center" as the
name of the organization, and we ultimately adopted "Queens Pride
House (a Center for the LGBT Communities of Queens)" instead.
My presence also subjected to further scrutiny the proposal that we
have one male and one female co-chair. I pointed out that, as someone
who identified as a male-bodied woman, it was not entirely clear to
me for which position my colleagues would consider me eligible
should they decide to elect me as chair. That same question came up
in April 2001 during the formation of the Out People of Color Political Action Club (OutPOCPAC) in New York City, a citywide political
organization for queer people of color. I suggested that our bylaws
simply reference the need for "gender balance" in the leadership of

the organization. When I was on the steering committee of Gay Asian & Pacific Islander Men of New York (GAPIMNY) during 1998-1999, I raised the issue of transgender inclusion in the mission of the organization, and the steering committee approved my proposal for a revision of the organization's mission statement to include trans-gendered men and women in addition to gay, bisexual, and questioning men of API descent.

As the only adoptee actively involved with Iban/Queer Koreans of New York, a group that I cofounded in February 1997, I encouraged people to include Korean adoptees in addition to Koreans and Korean Americans in the mission of the organization. And as the only openly transgendered person active in Also-Known-As (an organization of adult intercountry adoptees, mostly Korean adoptees) I was asked to edit a special LGBT issue of *TransCultured,* AKA's quarterly publication.

My difference as the only transgender-identified person of color among the founders of the New York Association for Gender Rights Advocacy has come to be of particular significance in our legislative work. NYAGRA was created in part to secure enactment of laws protecting transgendered and gender-variant people from discrimination and hate crimes. Since our founding in June 1998, we have launched three campaigns for transgender-specific and transgender-inclusive legislation. One was for transgender inclusion in the state hate crimes law enacted in July 2000, another was for transgender inclusion in the Dignity for All Students Act and a third was for passage of Int. No. 754, a bill that would amend the New York City human rights law to include gender identity and expression in the definition of gender, thereby protecting transgendered and gender-variant people from discrimination in the five boroughs. The campaign for Int. No. 754 took place in a city in which people of color constitute a majority—and a growing majority at that—of the population. As a transgendered person of color, I have made a special effort to reach out to communities of color in order to generate support for Int. No. 754 in the city council. Working in partnership with council members Bill Perkins (an LGBT-supportive African American from Harlem) and Margarita Lopez (a Latina lesbian from the Lower East Side), we have been able to gain the support of leading people of color in the city council, such as council member Guillermo Linares (a Dominican American from Washington Heights), the chair of the Black and Latino Caucus.

One of the difficulties I have encountered in my transgender activism has been in getting other transgender activists to take issues of race and ethnicity seriously. For example, at the press conference on the steps of city hall in February 2000, which initiated the public phase of the campaign for Int. No. 754, one politically prominent member of the NYAGRA board declared, "When I transitioned, I lost my white skin and my white skin privilege." I was shocked at the astonishing display of ignorance embodied in this comment from a white transsexual, and I was deeply embarrassed for the organization and the community that she should make such a declaration as she stood between two African-American city council members, one gay and one straight, and nearby one Latina lesbian Council member and the executive director of a leading Latino advocacy organization. My attempts to explain to her—in the most diplomatic manner possible—both the principle behind the strategy of seeking support from people of color in the council and the pragmatic politics of such a strategy was met with open hostility, and she said to me at one meeting, "Cut the people-of-color crap, Pauline; it's not working."

The problem at the national level is perhaps even more acute, as virtually the entire national leadership of the transgender political community is white, and most of the prominent activists are white male-to-female (MTF) transsexuals. One of the most disillusioning encounters I have had was with a white MTF transsexual woman, who is perhaps the most widely recognized transgender activist in the United States—though she has since come to reject the term "transgender" and the very notion of a transgender community. I was on the organizing committee for TransWorld, the first conference specifically by and for transgendered people of color anywhere, which was held in Brooklyn in October 1998. When I called this individual to invite her to participate in the conference, she responded with pique, labeling the conference a "racist" event because the organizing committee had decided to invite only people of color as formal guest speakers. I tried to explain to her that the conference was open to all, and that anyone could speak from the floor in a plenary session or participate in a workshop, but she persisted in her assertion that any conference that would not formally invite her as a guest speaker because she was white was inherently racist and exclusionary.

As these two incidents show, the unfortunate reality is that there are some people whom one may never reach. Sadly enough, it is quite common, in my experience, to encounter people who suffer under one form of oppression (in these two cases, transgenderphobia) who fail to recognize another form of oppression (in this case, racism, including their own racism).

Conversely, articulating my gender identity in nontransgender groups and organizations has often been a challenge as well. Most queer API groups are gender specific, and I have often found myself the only transgendered woman in what is essentially a gay men's group (though it might officially identify as a GBT organization) or the only transgendered woman in what is basically a lesbian group (though it might call itself an LBT organization). Many of the gay men in those groups "do drag," and it is some of those men who find me the most inexplicable or even threatening. What some gay men find particularly puzzling is my self-identification as a "male-bodied woman," neither a "drag queen" (a gay man who does "drag" occasionally for fun or entertainment) nor a transsexual (who seeks or has obtained sex reassignment surgery). Conversely, casual comments by some lesbians in women's groups often come in the form of little Freudian slips that suggest that the individuals making the comments do not view me as a "real" woman but rather as something else, perhaps some version of a gay man. One of the particular challenges of such queer API groups is to articulate my gender identity in a way that renders both my identity and my relationship to the group "political" in some meaningful sense.

Just as my authenticity as a woman is often in question in queer API groups, so too is my authenticity as an Asian. As an English-speaking Korean adoptee raised in a European-American household in the Midwest, I have not had the same integral connection with my culture of birth as do first-generation, 1.5-generation, and many second-generation Korean Americans. The lack of Korean-language proficiency and familiarity with (and perhaps more significantly, acceptance of) Korean cultural norms has limited my ability to do political work in Korean American communities. As a non–Korean-speaking transgendered Korean adoptee, I find that the novelty of my identity creates barriers to playing a more significant role in Korean American or Asian/Pacific American politics. That may be why I found special satisfaction in my experience giving testimony to the President's Advisory Commission on Asian Americans and Pacific Islanders at the eastern regional town hall meeting in September 2000 as a representative of GAPIMNY and, along with Christine Lipat of Kilawin Kolektibo, of a coalition of queer API organizations in the Northeast.

The task of community organizing is never an easy one, and it is especially difficult in more marginalized communities. I have seen some people succumb to the temptation to privilege their "own" oppression over those of others. In my activist work, I feel compelled to balance the need to serve particular communities who ostensibly share a common culture—as with ethnic-specific groups such as Iban/QKNY—with the need for broader formations, whether those be panethnic organizations (such as GAPIMNY) or multiracial organizations serving a specific geographic constituency (such as OutPOCPAC and Queens Pride House).

In my work in NYAGRA, I have attempted to articulate and maintain the broadest possible vision of gender oppression and therefore of gender liberation. My vision includes not only transgendered people but also nontransgendered gender-variant people, such as relatively masculine females who nonetheless identify as women and relatively feminine males who nonetheless identify as men. At the same time, my vision does not lose focus on the particular and particularly intense forms of oppression experienced by the most marginalized groups within that broader gender community.

The challenge that I see in all my activist work is to recognize and address the particular needs of particular communities while at the same time not succumbing to a particularism of philosophy or a parochialism of perspective. The call for a "postidentity politics" of gender made by one leading national transgender organization ignores the fundamental reality that many identities form in response to oppression. Clearly, "transgender" is a social construct, as is "Asian/Pacific American," "Korean adoptee," or any other identity label. But eliminating identity labels will do nothing to address the particular oppressions that gave rise to those identities in the first place. Rather, such identity formations can be used to construct communities and to organize such communities politically.

We live in an age of identity politics, in which a politics of difference can be used to unite or to divide. Certainly, some will be tempted to use difference to privilege one group over another or to pit one group against another. But a consciousness of difference need not necessarily exclude others; instead, it can be deployed strategically to bring about transformative social change. The challenge, as I see it, is to transcend the limits of identity politics in order to embrace a broader vision of a politics of difference. My activism and advocacy have been shaped by a lifelong consciousness of difference—*my* difference—and it informs my commitment to the empowerment of the communities with which I identify.

prelude and fugue in yellow and grey

k. terumi shorb

prelude

once upon a time
there was a little girl-boy
or a boy-girl
who lived in a castle
in the middle of suburbia

the little girl-boy knew
when she was very little
that when she grew up
she wanted to be a he

and this little girl-boy knew
that when she grew up
big little boys
would stop calling her
jap

if it was the last thing she did
and before the little girl-boy
could leave her body
or her face
her family left the country

to where she was no longer a jap
but a *gaijin* [foreigner]
no longer a girl-boy
but in fact
as much a girl as the next

fugue

with small hands, i slowly tie my windsor knot. something that i take great care in doing. it is my daily resistance. i, with my girlish body and round edges, feel the continuous scrutiny of my attire. i do my best to coordinate, using monotones sometimes, juxtaposing opposite chromatic schemes at other times. in many people's minds, i am a smartly-dressed man——until they hear me speak.

or until they see that angle of my back that is just too voluptuous, or the curve in my shoulders that is just not quite "guy."

"you tie that tie yourself?" a christian man asked me once, awkwardly grinning while trying to hide that he questioned my motives. "yes, everyday. i love the full windsor," i say, accentuating the daily ritual that unabashedly marks my appearance as queer.

a short asian man in a tie with a shirt that hugs his torso walks into the women's rest room. or is he she?

it is a reminder, to myself and all those who choose to call me "sir" or "um ..." that appearances can have many genders, and that not all of them need to be one or the other. it is kind of like the time when my lover and i stood on the corner across from fanatics singing hymns and holding signs reading "god hates fags." the caption in the paper the next day mysteriously read, "gay couple kiss in protest," leaving both of us to wonder whether they thought we were both men or they just didn't realize that "gay" does not always signify all queers.

a woman of color who had read my sixty-seven-page coming-out story/letter to my parents told me it was not radical enough. i had to talk about being oppressed as a person of color; about appropriation, exoticization, and exploitation. she, a straight person, did not realize that me, an asian american hapa (mixed-race) dyke, deciding to communicate honestly with my japanese mother about my sexuality was probably one of the most radical acts i had done. even amidst taking over campus administrative buildings, writing scathing letters to the editor about lack of staff of color, and calling my liberal professor a racist in front of an entire class, i had not gone that last step needed in order to implicate myself in the many layers of what is called oppression. one of the hardest things for me was confronting the oppression that faced me in my own home, with my own family.

as a child, my tiny hands would search my father's middle-class closet, stroking the silk ties and suits that smelled like smoke and shaving cream. this was decadence: something that i could only do when no one else would see. sometimes stumbling to pull a jacket off a hanger and feeling its weight, i dreamed of one day looking like my father going to work. always wanting my hair to be even shorter, i could only play with the boys, shedding stray glances at the snobbish white girls who never saw me and never would.

somehow my hapa identity played into my lack of trust for, but utter infatuation with, these white girls. they thought little of me and when they did, i was dirty; perpetually brown in the summer and gray-yellow-green in the winter, not to mention my chronic dressing pattern that was a mix between my mother's japanese uniformity (with matching sanrio top and bottom) and my almost relentless need to avoid all that was girly. streaks down my cheeks, i wanted those girls around me. i did not know at the time what more i would want even if they gave me the time of day. respecting them too much, i could not want them like i did the nude women in my juvenile fantasies that would touch me in my eight-year-old sleep.

it was scary; i knew so strongly and for so long what i liked and what i wanted that when i realized my stray glances and penis envy were wrong, i entered the eternal school of indecision. even once we moved to japan, where enforced school uniforms enabled my appearance to be less of an issue, i left the decisions to my mother, my friends, my teacher—hoping to hide my undying want to connect with girls.

it's an interesting mix-match: japanese american in japan, girl-wanting-girl in a country where holding hands is common as is sharing beds and baths. it was in this mix that i found someone to whom i could confess my love; a girl who had spent her childhood of unbelonging all across "america," yet commanded both japanese and english like a ruthless leader. she was all i wanted in me.

it was a discreet high school relationship. holding hands under the lecture desks, kissing each other in bathroom stalls, sneaking into her dorm room during the day. sometimes rumors would pop up, people spotting us kissing behind the gym, and one boy not telling her about his attraction because he was afraid of my probable jealousy. we liked the mystery. it was us against the world. we had no role models, no people like us, but we had each other and that was more than enough. we were happy, warm, and shy.

and then, after two and a half years, she left me for a bio-boy. as with so many queers, i became bitter with rage because she was entering what i saw as a hetero relationship, as if to annihilate what we had. the nineteen-year-old me could only accept this betrayal as evidence of my inadequacy; proof that male-female romance was the only answer and that our love had been wrong love, inferior love, even though we had seemed so happy for so long.

becoming an undergrad at an american college forced me to think about these things. i didn't want to. i thought that seeing my sexuality in a public light was so unabashedly "american." shameless, these americans, i would think. having recently become a *kibei* (a japanese american who lives in japan for a period of time and then returns to the united states) made my assumptions about all americans acutely negative. americans over-react, they are self-centered, immature, and oblivious. but not me. this is how i justified staying in the closet for two of my years at college.

in hindsight, i wonder about my arrogance. despite these feelings, i eventually came out to my family. still amazed, i wonder what prompted it. was it my then-prized but ignorant mentor who told me that it was ok for white people to wear kimonos and have dreadlocks, because people who want their culture treated with respect are "full of b.s."? how did that play into my coming to terms with being queer? was it because by fighting racist liberalism, i could no longer deny other parts of myself? was it the transformation from trying-to-assimilate asian girl to angry, confrontational person of color that forced me to reconcile all aspects of myself that were "different"? when did i decide to stop wearing anything that was deemed feminine? what did my female body sleeping with other female bodies have to do with my newly found necktie-wearing self? by coming out to my mother, was i becoming an "american"? was i denying my japanese identity, my japanese blood? how many times could i break my mother's heart?

we always look at coming out in layers. when do we choose to be out? to our lovers? our friends? our co-workers? our parents? do we out ourselves in the mall? at the chinese new year celebration? at the national conference on race and ethnicity? at the "free mumia" rally (to free mumia abu jamal from prison)? what do we choose to come out as? when do we leave what behind? sometimes a faggot, sometimes a tranny boy, sometimes just a lesbian. sometimes a dyke.

these questions haunt me. they are the bane of my existence, yet they are my bread and water. when i think about my daily rituals, the lines between the many experiences i have and their intersection with others are blurred. these questions force me to see my reflection, preventing my brain from erasing myself from the histories, the loves and loves lost, from the television set of the mind's eye. hearing testimonies, both my own and others, becomes more than just bearing witness. the response is visceral and tactile, like the sigh from the velvet skin of her back on my fingertips.

yet it nags. the knowledge that i'm not the only one crying, not the only one sighing. by coming out, i have stopped many tears (my own and others'), but i have created so many. i continue to choose to come out again and again: as different things, and in different ways, to different people and for different reasons. trying to find poetry in this identity battle is like buddhist monks screaming at the sea to crush their vocal chords: necessary, but sadly masochistic; liberating, but confining.

still, i wake up in the morning and tie my tie, knowing that i cannot fight everyone and can only free very few. this is my resistance, i say.

it is also my life.

coda

fatigued and weary
she wanders across the campus
where the politics were over-simplified

power dynamics were set in stone
and all morals were binary

tired of being tired
angry about being angry
she whispers to herself
it's not about who gets more and
who's "most oppressed"
it's about who doesn't get
and most of all
it's about
why

and in the over-liberalized mantra of
you can't please everyone
branded over and over in her mind
she must remind herself,
if you can't please everyone,
who exactly is being pleased?

yet the banner child of
her beloved movement
freedom!
she exclaims
only to find the criticism
continuously articulated as:
she's of color, she must be right
she's white, she must be wrong
writing off people as they would checks
with the ever-loving excuse of:
she's wac

she remembers amiri baraka saying
just because you're black
doesn't mean you're down
but tripping over her feet
she mumbles
there are struggles faced by
my own people,
every day, everywhere

seen as faceless, mindless
masses of people to sweep
under the rug

this isn't an individual issue
she screams as cold passersby
try to ignore their distress
it's about community,
realized or not
constructed or not
global or not
but it is an individual issue
she thinks
just wanting to remember
the community is there
to help the one person,
the one person is there
to help the community

what happens, when the community
refuses to back the one person
what happens, when the one person
refuses to be a part of the community

she writes
there shouldn't be anything inherently wrong
about people of color dating whites
but cringes,
there is something wrong about almost
every faculty of color having a white spouse

take a larger sample
they always say
large enough to tweak the numbers

* * *

my people die every day
she cries

yet i survive and eat and think and
love and learn and eat and think

knowing
that her survival is privilege
knowing
that her survival is blood money
knowing
that her survival is crucial
to the survival of her people

and exactly who are your people anyway
asked the teacher
sniffing with a smirk on his face
she begins a laundry list of:
people of color, asians, immigrants, queers, trans-folk, mixed-race
children, women....
and stops to say
it is those who have been raped or
killed or fired or ignored
our lives being shaped by the words
of a faceless, amorphous organism called
america, (amerikkka)
headed and controlled by the so-called
straight white man (rich to boot)
but aided and abetted by
non-straight-non-white-non-men
my people, who still refuse to keep the status of victim
though "we're half the world"
but still on the outside

she hesitates:
trying to prevent herself
from taking the easy
the black and white
the right and wrong
the gay and straight
(everything is one or the other)
she still says
there is truth to be found somewhere
there is life to be found somewhere

to defenestrate is to toss out
of a window
as she wished to do with all
the theory and lingo
she learned in classes
with the warm, passionate causes
locked in unwarm, unpassionate
term papers

but afraid she clings on
and rereads her thoughts
afraid she remembers
the lonely nights
of unbelonging
afraid she lies
in the unbrightness
of her room
her closet
her self

pushed back into whence she came
pulling all she cares for
back with her
she screams into a downward spiral
of self-hate, frustration, and guilt
awaking,
it becomes less unclear

it's not about me,
she hesitates
but it's all about me;
me helping you, so that
you can help me, so that
we don't forget why
we're here

and it's about
me loving you, so that
you can love me, so that

we can be
in the light
and in the fight
and live
and live

and live

15

Activism and Identity Through the Word: A Mixed-Race Woman Claims Her Space

Wendy M. Thompson

When I first heard that this book was being assembled, I felt compelled to write about my own experience and create a voice for myself and for people like me who struggle within margins. I wanted to reserve a place for myself within this space we call Asian/Pacific America. I wanted to speak out as a bisexual woman, a poor woman, a young woman, and a mixed-blood woman who has survived sexual violence. And I do so knowing that, for the most part, I cannot represent and will not fully be accepted by APA communities or queer communities because, within them, I often fall out of the boundaries for not being obviously either.

My skin color and appearance betray my Asian American identity. My identification as a bisexual person invites assumptions that I cannot make up my mind or that I am still questioning and will one day find my true sexual identity as either gay or straight. A certain stigma is attached to being both queer and Asian American: It just doesn't happen, or when it does, it's because the person has been Americanized and has adopted this freestyle form of "American" sexuality.

When identifying racially, I say that I am Afro-Chinese American. I may not be Chinese enough to compete for the title of Miss Chinatown, I may only be half-Chinese and exist without the super-Asian stereotypes and model-minority status, but I am an Asian American and no one can take that away from me. This is part of my activism: claiming my own agency and naming myself. I know it has been difficult for my mother, an immigrant who has lived throughout the Asian continent, to know herself and come close to claiming her own agency. It has been difficult for my African-American father who, in his own self-hatred and desire to become detached, raised his three daughters as Asian daughters, disregarding their brown skin.

I was born in Oakland, California, in 1981. It was an experimental time for all of us. My father was living post-Black Power Movement, struggling with menial jobs, with being a new father, and with trying to be a better father than his own abusive, alcohol-dependent dad. My mother was still learning what "America" was all about. She had been disowned for dating my father. With nowhere left to go, she married him and became pregnant with me. They raised me to be moral and religiously righteous. They raised me in hopes that I would not grow up to mimic the bad habits they had inherited from their parents. I was taught to be an obedient Chinese daughter because, at this time of urban, social, and economic decay, being black was more a burden than something to be proud of.

Growing up, I was reprimanded when I spoke of sex. My parents told me never to touch myself "down there" and raised me to reflect all aspects of what it meant to be a good woman who would someday become some man's wife. I never told anybody about my sexual explorations or how I felt about girls. Psychologists say it's normal for little children to experiment with the same sex while growing up, but at what age do they expect the child to grow out of it?

In school, I was called names and picked on for not acting like a regular girl. I remember being curious about pornography after sneaking looks at my father's *Playboys*. I told a girl friend about these girl-on-girl spreads and after recess had found that she had blabbed about it to the entire fifth-grade class. I was shamed and ostracized by the kids at school for being attracted to women and women's bodies. I had assumed that the boys disliked me so much and ridiculed me because I was ugly, weak, and wore secondhand clothes, not because I posed some kind of sexual threat to them. The girls avoided me altogether, afraid I'd try something on them. It was hard being branded a "lesbo" or "pervert" by my classmates, and being one of the few mixed-race people at my school only further complicated things.

The first time I ever knew of any girl who self-identified as a queer was in high school. There was a biracial girl I had known since tenth grade. From day one, she had always dressed like a tomboy, wearing basketball jerseys and baggy "boys" clothing. The girls she hung out with talked about her behind her back, gossiping that there was something wrong with her and she must be gay because of her nonfeminine mannerisms and lack of attraction toward boys. At the beginning of school the following year, when everyone was busy talking about their vacations, their new boyfriends, and other random happenings, she showed up in leather pants, combat boots, spiked collars, and her curly hair shaved off. The fashion statement was one thing, but she also made it verbally known that she was out. Once this happened, she was immediately ostracized by her old friends but quickly made new ones—the Goth kids who hung out alone for the same reasons— and began a new trend of experimental sexual encounters with some of the younger female students at school.

Watching her become brave and come out, I felt that there was no reason I should deny any part of who I was. It was as if in the past I had been living a secret life, or two secret lives: one as an undercover Chinese American girl and the other as an undercover girl who loved girls (and boys occasionally). In coming out sexually and coming to terms with my identity in a society obsessed with labels and categorization, there was always some kind of backlash from men who thought I was "not woman enough"; from (white) feminists who rejected my theories of having a feminism that was geared toward the "agenda" (that is, the mere survival and education) of women of color and poor women; from GLBTQ community organizations inside and outside of school that seemed to be dominated by white queers and in which I could never really feel accepted, only seen/treated as a token; and from my mother, whose sole want was for me to have a good life and to be a normal girl.

My activism springs from my own experiences with racism, with sexual and physical violence, and with sexism and homophobia. It springs from years of wanting but never feeling brave enough to combat these issues, and of putting off these encounters until I had gotten bigger, older, and wiser. But you can never put off these experiences. You get hurt, you bleed, you get angry, and you move on, but you never forget.

As a writer, an artist, and an activist, my identities and personal political beliefs are always infused into my work. I write and create mainly from the perspective of a queer mixed-race woman who is navigating her way through a world that criminalizes and incarcerates youth at increasingly higher rates (while youth crime rates are steadily dropping), that teaches girls to value and adhere to sick sexist gender roles, and that is unsafe for anyone existing publicly outside of the heterosexual mainstream.

I could march to city hall with placards in my hands chanting catchy slogans, but I believe that, for me, the best way to actively bring change is to carve it from the inside out. Through art, through writing, through other sources of media, my voice and agenda can be more effectively visualized and absorbed by those beyond my immediate community. I want people to experience my activism in ways other than by watching it televised on the evening news or reading about it in the newspaper. I want them to walk into a gallery or open up a book and feel captivated by the images. I want them to reflect on what they encounter, I want them to critique it, I want my visions and words to permeate their minds and make them really question their positions regarding gender, sexuality, class, and ethnicity.

The main goal of my art and activism is to steer marginalized people toward finding their voices, toward finding their places or creating a space in this society that they can call their own. I would like to see more queer/poor/urban/surviving youth and people of color representing themselves within media, literature, and the arts. Just because we see Lucy Liu's face in theaters and see Amy Tan's writings neatly shelved in bookstores doesn't mean that we—particularly in APA communities—have succeeded and that the job is done. There are a select number of sexual and ethnic representations out there but are they accurate? And if they're not, why not create our own?

I feel that I will always exist at the fringes of society. In being racially mixed I will never be assumed to be an Asian but always something else. In believing that sexuality is fluid and that no one should be forced to deny their love for a person because of their physical sex, I will constantly be regarded as a sexual rebel, a loose and dangerous woman. Being queer is being anything but normal, and being queer is what I would prefer to be, seeing that normality in this society comes at a painful price. I don't want to limit myself in any area. I want to love myself and other women the way I choose. I have the right to choose my community and home. I will cross borders and break boundaries because I was never an obedient girl to begin with and was always much too curious to "stay inside the lines."

Many people ask me, "Who are you and what are you doing here?"

They want to know who I am: What is my racial, ethnic, socioeconomic, sexual background?

And what I am doing here: Where am I from? Whose side am I on? How far do I intend to go?

My answer is that I am a complex individual who is simply trying to change the world. I am a woman yelling from the sidelines, creating new narratives, bringing forth a new experience, using her power to transform and fight and bring beauty to this society.

The following is a poem I wrote that describes the time around which I came out and the feelings of my community and family in response to this decision as well as my own feelings regarding my ever-shifting identity.

the first (culture fuck)

I saw her for the first time
Standing in front of a dressing-room mirror
Trying on a bathing suit that fit too loose over too small limbs
Her slant eyes bitter
Her mouth twisted down.
It was no accident
The disoriented Oriental
Outgrowing her place
Like a wild untamable stalk of sugarcane
Japanese Godzilla made in the USA
Towering over buildings
Water towers
Overturning vehicles and corrupting freeways.
For the first time I was seeing me
It was a distorted reflection
The half-black Asian girl
The only person darker than the super-smart FOB kids in my English honors class
Stuck at home on Friday nights
Only to turn 18 one day and leave home with plans for the prom.
My mother standing in the doorway
My father behind her
His fists balled up
Her mouth the shape of an O

A maddening scream in Mandarin
About
How dare I walk out the house wearing *that*
That!
They ache knowing that I am unstoppable
A little brown girl born out of broken English
Stuffing herself with *bao* and rice
While her immigrant mommy tells her:
be a good girl
be polite
study hard
and smile.
Yet I was not good enough
I was not polite
And I didn't study hard.

My aunts wanted me to be pretty
They fed me lies at my *po po's* (grandmother's) house about how
If I ate all the *bok choi* on my plate
I would one day be Miss Chinatown
With a diamond tiara stranded in my curly black hair
The sash covering a chest where big American breasts should be
I was never as good-looking as I should have been.

But I was the number-one daughter
No sons
Just three girls
Bad luck
And arguing.
Ma crumpling to the floor after daddy hits her in the head with the
door of the freezer
I hated that refrigerator ever since.
Black daddy yelling at yellow mommy about not understanding
English
Stupid motherfucker, he says
I act like I don't hear it.
I don't hear a lot of things
The way my father is disappointed for not having a son
And in my act to appease him

He calls me stupid
Confused
He says I am needing therapy
Because I act like a man (dysfunctional)
All macho
Pretending I do not know how to cry.
I talk loud and mask my body with XXL clothes
I make myself look bigger than I am.
Act like the tough guy and challenge boyfriends to fights
Coming home with a smashed nose
Bloody black eyes.
I do not report it when they rape me
The first and the next
Proving that they are real men
Realer than my fake acts of survival.
They get offended when I say I like girls
They feel threatened
And establish the boundaries by saying that I will never have a dick to
please her with.
My sesame-seed girl on top of my brown-rice body.
They say she won't fall for it,
Bullshit.
But still we act it out
Like genderfucked Barbie dolls
Me being the man-woman
And her
This girl with the Sanrio fetish who likes to buy tapioca drinks from
Chinatown
Her round moon face
Her body twisting like a root inside and outside of mine
Bending out of tradition.
She is not straight but won't admit she's gay either
Her sex split in halves like her culture
1.5 Korean American female sexed with laced thoughts of me
Undercover from her immigrant mother who can't quite roll the R's.

And I remember it like the first day we met
Or the first day I looked at her and we kissed.
She wasn't like the other girls,

She didn't pull away.
I remember how we faked it
Told her mom we were going upstairs to try on a new dress
When her mother suddenly burst into her bedroom and found me
doing *that*
That!
To her daughter
Spread-eagled and naked from the waist down
That!
It was no longer funny
The language had ceased
Our little fling ended with the shunning of my disloyal identity.
I had ruined that chance to prove my Asianness
To disown the part of me that was rotten
The apple that Buddha never blessed.
Turning mute
The eyes growing accustomed to the dark
Her two eyes never seeing that way again.
And after her disappearance they all became white
Like white walls and white sheets
White lovers like buttered popcorn and candy apple numbing my
tongue,
Scarring my taste.
No more fish balls snapped up in cross-legged chopsticks rubbing
together like lovers
The dim sum passed up for a meal of fast food burgers and fries.
I walk this world alone
Seeing signs in Spanish that hang in the greasy windows of Little
Asia Chinese Take-Out
Now serving American cuisine
Curtains browned and shut
Like her legs
And her mind.
A whispered reminder of how
English was never spoken here.

– 16 –

Things Come When Least Expected

"You Yun"

It all started in that spring afternoon, 1993, toward the end of my first year in a graduate program in psychology. It was my second year in the United States, and I had finally begun to feel that English was a language rather than a bunch of formulas to memorize. Warm and a little sleepy, I entered a classroom to attend a workshop on bisexuality. Times had certainly changed.

Born in 1960, I grew up in what was arguably the most sexually repressive period in the history of China. Many people were persecuted and falsely persecuted for sexual activity outside of legal marriages. From a very young age, I learned the importance of doing whatever it took to conform to a narrowly defined norm. And, upon seeing that my extended family never turned its back on any of my relatives who were politically persecuted, I also learned the importance of acceptance.

In the late 1970s, I was lucky enough to get into college, and it was there that I heard the word "homosexual" spoken for the first time. This experience also exposed me to popular responses to same-sex attraction, as when a classmate responded, "It's very cruel!" At the time, I didn't understand what she meant. Perhaps she thought that the person's homosexuality was "cruel" because it hindered the chance for reproduction, the most important privilege for any "natural" and healthy adult. Whatever the case, the word "cruel" stuck in my mind.

It reminded me of the first gay man I knew. A relative of mine was showing me the diary of a good friend of hers, which she suspected the friend wanted her to find. As we read it, we were shocked by the narration of his sexual encounters with other men and his frustration with not being able to develop a stable relationship with any of them.

I remember feeling sad that he would not have a chance to form a family and have offspring. I even remember thinking of trying to get him "cured," only to be told that the "passive type" of male homosexuals such as he would be very hard to cure. In the end, we felt that all that we could do for him was to keep his secret, and not even tell him that we knew.

Learning to embrace different sexualities has been a long process for me. Even after learning intellectually that judging individuals based on their sexuality is a form of discrimination, and even after learning socially to value people I knew were gay or lesbian, I nonetheless continued to feel that LGBT people were "strange" and shameful. For example, one of my professors, Professor W, came out on the first day of class, but I did not know what to do when I saw her female partner for the first time. I later wrote a note to Professor W explaining that I felt bad about my initial response. She responded in kind, expressing an appreciation to me for my openness: "Many heterosexual people feel uncomfortable in the presence of same-sex couples not so much because of their sexuality but because of a belief that same-sex couples somehow should feel vulnerable and shameful." I was learning to challenge my own internalized homophobia.

Which brings me back to the workshop. At one point, one of the speakers said that after coming out as an adult, she was able to reflect on her high school years and realize that her feelings for other girls were feelings of attraction. Suddenly, I remembered a moment when I was five years old in a classroom at my boarding nursery school one spring afternoon. The kids around me were playing with their toys. I was bored. I turned my head to the window, and when I saw other kids exercising in the yard, my eyes focused on a pretty girl in that group who caused a subtle feeling to go through my body.

This was not the first time that I, as an adult, had recalled this experience. In the early 1980s, when people in China began to break taboos and talk about sexuality, one of the popular topics of conversation was Freud's theory of children and a subsequent debate over whether or not they had sexual feelings. My experience suggested to me that children do have sexual feelings. But it was not until the workshop that I had ever questioned why my feelings were for another girl!

The loud applause woke me up. The workshop finished. I felt silly, and remember thinking to myself, "Like some first-year medical school students who feel they have almost all of the diseases they are learning about, I feel that I have all of the mental conditions I am learning about." However, every few weeks these questions came back to me, despite my attempts to ignore them. These issues even arose in my dreams. As the months passed, I knew that something was there. As one Chinese saying puts it, "Paper can't wrap fire." During that period, I sometimes wondered, "So, I'm not going to be the same as everybody else?" At other times I asked myself, "If you believe in Taoist philosophy, which accepts the nature of things, and you know your being attracted to women is natural, why can't you accept it?"

My internal struggles culminated on a cold night last fall, when I woke up from another nightmare and finally admitted to myself, "It's true. That's it." I felt both relieved and newly burdened, as if suddenly realizing that I was walking around carrying a huge mountain that was invisible to the people around me. The mountain was so heavy that a couple of times I had found myself wanting to leave this world to escape it. I knew that I needed to talk to somebody. It took me ten minutes to write down the first sentence of a note to Professor W: "I might be a lesbian or bisexual." And then before I knew it: "But I'm not ready to talk about it, so please do not bring it up until I myself do so."

When we eventually spoke about it, I waited for Professor W to reassure me by saying things such as, "It's okay to be a lesbian." Instead, she sat there, listening. Initially, I felt unsupported by her, though in a later conversation I learned why. She said, "I wanted to find out what's really going on with you, didn't want to assume, like some people do, 'oh, here's another one coming!'" I bring her statement with me everywhere I go in both my personal and professional life.

While in graduate school, I saw many LGB students strongly denounce homophobia in various classes and workshops. So, I was hesitant to talk to them since I was afraid that, since I had a hard time accepting myself, I would be seen as homophobic. But one day I saw B, the organizer of the LGB student group on campus, in the student lounge. I decided to tell him about my struggle. He listened. And when I mentioned my hesitation in speaking with others, he shook his head, smiled gently, and said, "No, no, no. We all came from there." A week later, I noticed that the feature article in the weekly newsletter of the LGB student group, written by B, sounded as though he was talking specifically to me. Indeed, the next time I saw B, he said, "I wrote it for you." We shared a bear hug. And I felt that my way of relating to the world and to other LGBT people was changing.

But I did not know where to find the LGBT community outside of school. I remembered hearing about something called a "coming-out group," and joined one in the spring of 1994. To my surprise, most people in the group went through a path similar to mine. For the first time, I felt I was not alone. Then I met the first Chinese lesbian I was to know in that city. Neither of us was a bar-goer, but we drove to all of the major lesbian bars in town to search for other Asian lesbians. We almost never found one, but we did eventually find a group, PALs (Pacific Asian Lesbian and Bisexual Women Network), and joined right away, which led to our finding even more groups for LGBTs as well as the first Midwest Asian lesbian and bisexual women's retreat in Minneapolis in 1995. Professionally, I noticed that a LGB division (the Society for the Psychological Study of Gay, Lesbian, and Bisexual issues) existed in the American Psychological Association (APA), and I joined that too.

Coming out as an adult had its own challenges. It seems to me that coming to understand one's sexuality in adulthood is different from knowing one's sexuality all along. I felt something totally new, even foreign, in my sense of self when I interacted with the people I had known for a long time. I felt as though they were not talking with the person they thought they knew, and that the real me had become a phantom. Primarily for this reason I started coming out to some old friends, both inside and outside China. The range of responses has been broad, from "How come you have become an American?" or "You just haven't found the right man" to "Congratulations for knowing yourself better!"

This process of coming out to more and more people planted the seed of my activism. In 1994, a friend of mine invited me to contribute to a magazine he edited. I wrote a couple of articles, including the story of a psychologist who was also a professor at my school and who happened to be bisexual. I wanted to show the human side of a psychologist, including her journey coming out.

Early in 1995, a psychologist in China introduced me to Wan Yan Hai, a health educator who was known internationally for his advocacy for the LGBT population and AIDS patients, as well as for his dedication to HIV/AIDS education in China. I was grateful for the connection because I had been wanting to meet more LGBT people who were in or from mainland China and who perhaps shared more of my experiences. Immediately, I wrote a short response to an article by an older gay man who had undergone many hardships during political movements from the 1950s to the 1970s and managed to stay single despite all of the pressures from his family and others. In the article, the man advised other gay people to avoid doing three things: disclosing their gay identity; complaining about the hardships caused by being gay; and entering a heterosexual marriage. I respected his experience, but felt his advice was misleading. In my response, I addressed the damage extreme isolation could cause, the necessity for people to air their grievances, and the importance of not judging gay people who needed heterosexual marriage due to their life circumstances.

I also made one-on-one connections when Wan referred to me a gay man in China who had been beaten repeatedly. The young man was reacting severely to the trauma he suffered not long ago, and I became concerned that he might commit suicide. I wrote to him, expressed my sympathy and empathy for him, and shared with him information on the impact of traumatic events on people's lives, hoping a better understanding of his experiences would help him cope and reduce the misperception that something was wrong with him as a person. Later he told me that my correspondence with him was one of the things that kept him alive at that difficult time.

In December 1994 some scholars in China held a symposium in Beijing that addressed various issues on homosexuality and the LGBT population in an affirming and accepting manner. Encouraged by their success, they decided to hold another conference at the end of 1995. To help, a friend and I publicized the conference in local gatherings and in the LGBT press (which otherwise carried little news about China), and even raised some funds. The conference was postponed indefinitely by the police, but the experience was a significant entry for me into community organizing, which continued when I helped with the first lesbian conference in China in 1998.

As my involvement in the community was deepening, I started getting concerned about the possible impact of my activism on my family. I came out to my sister in 1994, and it caused her great distress. Her distress was eased by her getting to know gay communities in

China, but she did not want me to come out to our parents for fear that they would get hurt. My response was that I was active in LGBT community work and didn't want our parents to hear anything from anybody other than me—especially something that could be shocking and even harmful. Reluctantly, my sister agreed to work with me. I wrote a letter and made an audiotape for my parents. A lot of communication and miscommunication occurred, but eventually the situation was resolved, and my activism continued.

In the fall of 1995, I was invited to contribute to the first anthology on the lives of mainland Chinese LGBTs. I did. I told the story about my coming out to myself and my family, and shared information about LGBT communities I found in the United States and about the success story of a friend who not only found her love, but also established a stable family. I wanted to tell my sisters and brothers in China that it's possible for us to live a "normal" life.

In the summer of 1996, to establish more professional connections, I started looking for Chinese mental health professionals who already had contact with the APA regarding LGBT issues. I found that such communication had yet to happen, and that similarly, LGBT psychologists in the United States knew little about LGBT issues in China. I learned that the APA Public Interest Office had a lot of publications on various issues which they distributed free of charge, including the APA Policy Statements on LGB issues and research on psychotherapy for LGB clients, but that the gay-friendly professionals and activists in China did not know about these resources. I assumed there had been a bridge between the APA and China and that I would simply need to join those people to continue the work, but this bridge had not yet been built. So, I sent the APA publications to China, and Wan and his friends had them translated, published in their newsletter, and posted on the Internet. I tried to translate each piece I received from China into English and post it on an APA electronic mailing list and other lists. I didn't think I had done all that much until some people I met in conferences asked me, "How do you find time to do your homework?" No wonder I felt so tired sometimes!

I started to do more educational outreach in the APA. At their 1997 convention, I presented on LGBT issues in China and the revision of the *Chinese Classifications of Mental Disorders* (which then still classified homosexuality as a sexual disorder). In 1998, I did another presentation at the APA convention in which I gave an update on LGBT issues in China. I also became more involved in other organizations, including two groups that I helped to establish: the Lavender Phoenix and the Chinese Society for the Study of Sexual Minorities (CSSSM). In the summer of 1998, I presented on behalf of these two groups at the Chinese *Tongzhi* (the Mandarin term for all sexual minorities) Conference and at the Second National Asian and Pacific Islander Lesbian and Bisexual Women's Conference. How did I go about establishing these groups?

On Labor Day weekend of 1997, after seven months of deliberation, some of us gathered in Los Angeles and formed CSSSM. Our goals were the depathologizing of homosexuality and the building of LGBT communities in China. For various reasons, we did not work as a group for long, but we became good friends and supported one another in our individual efforts toward these goals. The most successful project was the CSSSM biweekly Internet magazine, *Tao Hong Man Tian Xia* (which literally means "pink color all of the world," denoting we are everywhere), edited by Eryan Lin and posted at <http://www.csssm.org>. It's one of the oldest Chinese gay Web pages, one of the few educational and very informative ones, and one that has been influential in Chinese tongzhi communities. Another successful project was asking the APA to send a letter to the Chinese Psychiatric Association to support the depathologization of homosexuality in their third edition of the *Chinese Classifications of Mental Disorders,* which the APA did send.

Lavender Phoenix, a network for lesbian, bisexual, and questioning women in and from mainland China, was established in May 1997 by five women in the United States who met each other, in person or electronically, in our separate searches for a community. We invited not only lesbian, bisexual, and questioning women in and from China, but also all women who were interested in our issues, regardless of their race, ethnicity, and sexual orientation. We set up an e-mail discussion list that has grown in size from five to more than seventy participants. We have shared information with one another, had serious discussions on coming out and community building, supported one another during difficult times, and made good friends. We have even managed to get together roughly once a year, usually in some member's home. In 2001, for the first time, we needed to rent a bigger space for our gathering.

Looking back, I see my journey into activism as a mixture of home-coming and coincidence. Coming out to myself as a lesbian started out to be one of the most frightening experiences in my life, but surprisingly, turned out to be one of the most liberating and growth-facilitating ones. Opportunities to speak out to larger and larger audiences happened to come at times when I was ready to speak. At the time, all I thought I wanted was to break my isolation. I once read that some people publish books because they couldn't find the kind of books they were looking for. I never thought the same thing could happen to me. But now I know that such things really can happen to anybody.

I've learned much about myself in this journey, and not simply about my sexual orientation. I've learned about the strength and ability that I didn't know that I had, my limitations and vulnerabilities, as well as my passions and beliefs. All of this gives me a better sense of direction for my future, professionally as well as personally. As well, all of this has made this journey a very healing one for me. Growing up in the 1960s and 1970s in China, I internalized various stigmas and other judgmental beliefs. After many years, I am learning to remove them one by one.

For me, participating in tongzhi community building blends broader social justice with my own personal growth. I don't think the concept of "queer" people would have any meaning outside the context of our current culture. I believe that homosexuality is as natural a part of human sexuality as heterosexuality, and the only reason that same-sex attraction is a big deal is that it has been misunderstood. People who express it have been and still are being discriminated against. I believe that we LGBTs can be really free only when the entire society accepts us, and I want to be part of the force that makes society a more accepting place.

Out on the Front Lines

Helen Zia

It was difficult for my parents to accept that I quit medical school to become a community organizer. I could hardly explain it myself, but I finally concluded that medicine was not right for me. The hardest part of my decision was letting my parents down. My mom said softly, "I hoped you would take care of me when I get old." My father stopped speaking to me for a time, which spared me from having to break the additional news that I was working as a construction laborer in the South End of Boston, at a site only a few blocks from my apartment.

In my new life, I was part of a fellowship of Asian American, Black, and Latino community and labor organizers working to integrate the highly paid construction trades, a tight fraternity long open only to white men. We saw ourselves as sisters and brothers on a journey toward a noble goal. Beyond the idealism, there was another upside: Paid at union scale, I made ten times more as a laborer than I had as a highly trained medical student. I could finally send some money home to my family, allowing me to make small contributions toward my filial obligations.

Construction work and union organizing were male-dominated arenas, as was medicine. The dynamics reinforced my belief that women should not have to wait in line for our liberation, no matter what Confucius or my Americanized cohorts said. I became deeply involved in Boston's burgeoning women's movement. Hundreds of women came to each meeting we organized that linked women's lives

"Out on the Front Lines" from "Moving the Mountain" from *Asian American Dreams: The Emergence of the American People* by Helen Zia. Copyright © 2000 by Helen Zia. Reprinted by permission of Farrar, Straus and Giroux, LLC.

with freedom struggles everywhere. I found a community of sisters, some of whom were openly lesbian. As I learned from the widely diverse range of women about their paths to self-awareness, I began to explore feelings that I'd had for a long time, that I was a lesbian.

Soon I was invited to a special meeting by my fellow Asian American and Black community activists. When I arrived at the meeting, I was seated at one side of the room, and my friends sat in a semicircle facing me. It slowly dawned on me that I was the subject of the meeting.

Tariq, a soft-spoken African-American man who led a collective of activists in the Roxbury neighborhood of Boston, started the discussion. "Helen, we've noticed that you're spending a lot of time with lesbians. We need to know if you're a lesbian, because you would harm our organizing efforts. We would have to break off ties with you and the other Asian Americans." It seemed wrong that my sexual orientation would reflect badly on everyone who looked like me, but my Asian American friends nodded in agreement. The leader of our Asian American group hastened to reassure Tariq. "Homosexuality is not part of our community," he said. "It's a symptom of white, middle-class self-indulgence. We could not have a lesbian working with us." The meeting became more like a trial as they amassed the charges and the evidence. Together, they asked how I would plead. "So tell us, Helen, are you a lesbian?"

I couldn't believe my ears. These friends, my extended family, were asking me to choose between my Asian American self and another intrinsic part of me. Feeling their stares as they awaited my response, I felt unsure. I hadn't acted on my impulses. Was I really a lesbian? I didn't know the answer, but I was certain of one thing. My Chinese upbringing taught me to value my family above all. Suddenly my extended family, my community, was threatening to disown me. Was I a lesbian? I answered, "No, I'm not."

Tariq and the others were relieved not to lose one of their energetic young organizers. The meeting was over and everyone went on to business as usual. Except for me. I had stepped into the closet and slammed the door shut. Rather than face my lesbian friends, I gradually stopped going to the women's gatherings. When friends in Detroit suggested I move there to discover America's heartland, I jumped at the chance.

In Detroit, what I found seemed to fill the void. As an autoworker at Chrysler, I experienced the essential humanity of people, across differences of race, culture, and class. I discovered my voice and my calling as a journalist. I embraced a vibrant Asian American community that went far beyond my fellowship of well-meaning activists. My work on the Vincent Chin case (reporting the events of this hate crime) cemented a deep relationship with my extended family of Asian Americans. Even my mother and father were proud of me— my shortcomings as a daughter and medical school dropout were forgotten.

Yet something wasn't right with me. I was still searching for a way to make my whole self welcome in my community of Asian Americans. After nearly a decade in Detroit, I moved back East to New York—to pursue my career as a magazine editor, to be closer to my family, and to find the person I had run away from.

There was no lack of Asian American activity in the New York I returned to. While I had been stamping out car parts and writing about the local Detroit scene, bustling communities of South Asians, Koreans, and Filipinos had sprung up. There seemed to be more new Vietnamese restaurants in Chinatown than Chinese. Hate crimes against Asian Americans were on the rise, as were boycotts of Korean American markets. I became part of a support network of Asian American women activists; I joined a growing effort to fight domestic violence in the Asian American community by volunteering with the New York Asian Women's Center. An exciting organization of Asian American journalists was starting in New York. My own career flourished—I was the editor in chief of a travel magazine, and later the executive editor of *Ms. Magazine.*

In another, separate part of my life, I had met someone to make a home with—and she was a woman. I came out as a lesbian. My life was full and happy, but it took on that strange bifurcation that many gay people experience. I was an Asian American and I was a lesbian, but in those days I couldn't be both in the same space. It was easy to maintain a facade in a world that presumed all Asian Americans to be heterosexual, and all gays to be white and generally male. Yet my commitment as a journalist and activist was to bring forward communities struggling for visibility. The contradiction grew increasingly intolerable.

When I came out to my family, they were loving and supportive, glad that I found happiness in a home life of my own. Mom talked about gays in old Shanghai and encouraged me to raise a family anyway. Aunt Betty in Queens continued trying to match me with Mr. Right. "So what if you're gay? You can still find a man," she said with a shrug. The remaining challenge was to come out to an Asian American community whose kinship meant so much, when memories of my lesbian trial and the threat of ostracism were still fresh.

An opportunity arose when I was to deliver a speech on Asian Americans and the media to the annual convention of the Asian American Journalists Association in 1992. It was a time when anti-gay campaigns were under way across the country, and Asian Americans seemed irrelevant to the national debate. I wanted to acknowledge that Asian Americans had a stake in the issue, but try as I might, I couldn't work sexual orientation into my short speech. So I asked Hayley, the emcee and a friend, to add this minor detail to her introduction. Fine, no problem, she said. As Hayley addressed the national gathering of journalists and the live C-SPAN cameras, she said, "Helen is a longtime journalist, a feminist and . . ." She hesitated, stammering. "And she's a l-l-l-lesbian . . ." She paused to adjust the microphone and asked, "Did you all hear that? She's a l-l-l-lesbian. . . ."

My fear of losing my ties to the Asian American community never materialized. Rather, I discovered a new sense of freedom with my colleagues and my work. In a small way, my televised coming out was a statement that Asian Americans are everywhere in American life and belong in every aspect of national discourse. It was hardly a novel idea, but its time had come.

Afterword

I am so pleased to be a part of this collection of inspiring autobiographical stories by queer Asian/Pacific Americans. As I read the chapters of the book, I was struck by the honesty, self-reflection, and courage of the contributors. "Life is complicated" goes the opening line of Avery Gordon's *Ghostly Matters,* and by that she is referring to the ways in which layers of identity and oppression are seen as well as unseen (but nonetheless felt). The stories of queerness in this book more than bear out Gordon's claim about life's complications.

These stories, especially when taken together, are a refusal of the impulse to separate queer from Asian/Pacific Islander and both of these from everything else. As Kumashiro notes in the preface, the refusal is a restorying—an acknowledgement of difference without submission to the conventional narratives about difference. Sexuality and race, among other kinds of identity, touch on issues of social justice. We usually think of social justice as operating above the individual, in other words, social justice as a society-wide issue having to do with law, government, and policy. But social justice is, in my view, very much a matter of the self.

Although I am a generation apart from most of the contributors, our stories are similar. Our stories are about wanting to be seen in our wholeness. Indeed, being seen, being recognized, is a crucial part of our stories. But recognized as whom? It seems that when we are recognized by others, we are often only partially recognized. We are recognized as queer in one place and as Asian/Pacific American in another place. And sometimes, less occasionally than we would like, we are recognized in our entirety. But however we are recognized, as many of the contributors to this volume lament, the self often seems divided into different communities of interest.

There is something worthy of notice here. Recognition is not simply the condition of being seen, or even of being granted a political or legal right. Legal and political rights, as so many political scientists and philosophers have noted, are crucial forms of recognition produced through liberal democracy. But I am referring here to a sense of recognition that is deeper and more profound than what is promised by liberalism. It seems to me that the kind of recognition storied by these writers is a deep longing about others as well as about ourselves.

Who recognizes and who is recognized? I suggest here that being seen involves others as well as ourselves. Of course virtually everyone would agree that in an act of recognition, an Other sees and acknowledges another. Indeed, much activism is oriented towards changing the conventions, ideologies, and discourses uttered by others that we find repressive, limiting, and unjust. Social movements help transform prejudice into tolerance by changing ideas and selves. But perhaps it is less obvious that this activism is already linked to the self. What I mean by this is that, in effect, there is another aspect to recognition: the self-recognizing itself. Activism changes our own sense of self. Of course, I can hear some of you saying, "There is nothing wrong with me" or "The problem is not me but them," and so on.

I digress for a moment with a story. Last year, while crossing the college plaza near my office, a young Asian American student approached me. "Want to rush a fraternity?" he asked while thrusting a flyer toward me. "Oh, I don't think so," was my reply. My first blush of humiliation turned to a bit of anger. If it was funny that Mr. Fraternity thought I was twenty-five years younger than I am, the gender mistake didn't seem funny at all. Gender norms exasperate me because they discipline us in both conscious and unconscious ways. But the anger in my mind was different from the visceral response of my body. I felt my chest sink; my shoulders drew together as if my autonomic system tried to be small. The feeling of shame is unmistakable. To get away from the pain of it, my mind worked on a story: Mr. Fraternity is ignorant, the world is too straight, forget about it. But, and I have learned this the hard way, my body holds my deepest truth. There are times when no matter how hard we try, the mind cannot make it so. There is not a quick fix for this—but I know that being seen and recognized as queer, API, and all else, is not simply about how the Other sees us.

So when Kumashiro speaks of restorying, I think especially of a kind of recognition of the self that comes not from our stories (which are created by our minds) but from someplace deeper. That "someplace deeper" is likely to be different for different people. But for most us, getting to that place requires that we meet our selves and our stories. And when the self meets the self in the deepest possible way, there is a profound moment in which the stories—about what "they" do to us, and what "we" return to them—fall away.

Dana Y. Takagi
University of California, Santa Cruz

Dana Y. Takagi is currently an associate professor of sociology and the associate director of the Center for Justice, Tolerance, and Community at the University of California, Santa Cruz. Her primary research interests are in the areas of race and rights, nationalism, and most recently, the politics of progressive faith-based movements. She is also an editor of the UC Press series, *American Crossroads*.

Index

Out People of Color Political Action
    Club (OutPOCPAC), 94, 98
OutPOCPAC, 94, 98

Pacific Asian Lesbian and Bisexual
    Women Network (PALs), 122
PALs, 122
Parents
    hiding queerness from, 2
    isolated, feelings of, 48-49
    supportive, 2, 45-46
Parents, Families, and Friends of
    Lesbians and Gays (PFLAG),
    48, 50
PFLAG, 48, 50
Perkins, Bill, 95
Poetry, 101-110, 115-118
Postidentity politics, 98
Pride, strike of, 90
Proposition 21, 30
Proposition 22, 30
Proposition 187, 30
Proposition 209, 30
Proposition 227, 30
Protect Our Constitution, 14

Queens Lesbian and Gay Community
    Center, 94
Queens Pride House, 94, 98
Queer Coalition, 11

Racism, 7-9, 56, 79-80
Recognition, 131-132
Resistance, strike of, 90
Restorying, *xxiii, xxv*, 132

Retreat, Midwest Asian lesbian
    and bisexual women's, 122
"Rice queens," 75

SALGA, 12
Same-sex marriage, ban on, 14
"Save our State" initiative, 30
Self-hatred, 8, 10, 73-76
"Sex machine," 51
Shepherd, Reginald, 7, 9-10
Silahis, 23
Soap, 53
Social justice, literature, *xxiv*
South Asian Lesbian and Gay
    Association (SALGA), 12
"South of Normal," 53, 57
Standing Policies 1 and 2 (SP-1
    and SP-2), 31
Success, mask of, 59-62

Takagi, Dana Y., 131-133
Tao Hong Man Tian Xia, 125
Tongzhi, 125
TransCultured, 95
Transgendered, 93-99
TransWorld, 96
Tunnel vision, 34

Vegetarianism, 38
Victim blaming, racism, 79-80

"White disease," queerness as, *xxi*

SPECIAL 25%-OFF DISCOUNT!

Order a copy of this book with this form or online at:

http://www.haworthpress.com/store/product.asp?sku=4881

RESTORIED SELVES

Autobiographies of Queer Asian/Pacific American Activists

_____in hardbound at $29.96 (regularly $39.95) (ISBN: 1-56023-462-8)

_____in softbound at $12.71 (regularly $16.95) (ISBN: 1-56023-463-6)

Or order online and use special offer code HEC25 in the shopping cart.

COST OF BOOKS_____

OUTSIDE US/CANADA/
MEXICO: ADD 20%_____

POSTAGE & HANDLING_____
*(US: $5.00 for first book & $2.00
for each additional book)
Outside US: $6.00 for first book)
& $2.00 for each additional book)*

SUBTOTAL_____

IN CANADA: ADD 7% GST_____

STATE TAX_____
*(NY, OH & MN residents, please
add appropriate local sales tax)*

FINAL TOTAL_____
*(If paying in Canadian funds,
convert using the current
exchange rate, UNESCO
coupons welcome)*

Prices in US dollars and subject to change without notice.

☐ **BILL ME LATER:** ($5 service charge will be added)
(Bill-me option is good on US/Canada/Mexico orders only;
not good to jobbers, wholesalers, or subscription agencies.)

☐ Check here if billing address is different from
shipping address and attach purchase order and
billing address information.

Signature_____

☐ **PAYMENT ENCLOSED: $**_____

☐ **PLEASE CHARGE TO MY CREDIT CARD.**

☐ Visa ☐ MasterCard ☐ AmEx ☐ Discover
☐ Diner's Club ☐ Eurocard ☐ JCB

Account #_____

Exp. Date_____

Signature_____

NAME_____

INSTITUTION_____

ADDRESS_____

CITY_____

STATE/ZIP_____

COUNTRY_____ COUNTY (NY residents only)_____

TEL_____ FAX_____

E-MAIL_____

May we use your e-mail address for confirmations and other types of information? ☐ Yes ☐ No
We appreciate receiving your e-mail address and fax number. Haworth would like to e-mail or fax special
discount offers to you, as a preferred customer. **We will never share, rent, or exchange your e-mail address
or fax number.** We regard such actions as an invasion of your privacy.

Order From Your Local Bookstore or Directly From
The Haworth Press, Inc.
10 Alice Street, Binghamton, New York 13904-1580 • USA
TELEPHONE: 1-800-HAWORTH (1-800-429-6784) / Outside US/Canada: (607) 722-5857
FAX: 1-800-895-0582 / Outside US/Canada: (607) 771-0012
E-mailto: orders@haworthpress.com
PLEASE PHOTOCOPY THIS FORM FOR YOUR PERSONAL USE.
http://www.HaworthPress.com   BOF03